Also by Melanie Thernstrom

THE DEAD GIRL

Sinedu Tadesse
1974–1995
This is the photograph Sinedu sent
to *The Harvard Crimson* shortly
before her death.

Trang Phuong Ho
1974–1995
This is the photograph
commemorating Trang in the Shrine
at the Vietnamese Unity Buddhist
Temple in Boston.

Halfway Heaven

DIARY OF A
HARVARD MURDER

Melanie Thernstrom

DOUBLEDAY
New York   London   Toronto   Sydney   Auckland

PUBLISHED BY DOUBLEDAY
a division of Bantam Doubleday Dell Publishing
Group, Inc.
1540 Broadway, New York, New York 10036

DOUBLEDAY and the portrayal of an anchor with a
dolphin are trademarks of
Doubleday, a division of Bantam Doubleday Dell
Publishing Group, Inc.

Book Design by Jennifer Ann Daddio

Library of Congress Cataloging-in-Publication Data
Thernstrom, Melanie, 1964–.
Halfway heaven : diary of a Harvard murder / Melanie
Thernstrom.
p.   cm.
1. Murder—Massachusetts—Case studies.   2. Tadesse,
Sinedu.   3. Ho, Trang Phuong, 1974-1995.
I. Title.
HV6533.M4T48   1997
364.15′23′097444—dc21   97-8278
                                          CIP
ISBN: 0-385-48745-2

September 1997

First Edition

1   3   5   7   9   10   8   6   4   2

For Thao Nguyen

Lalefew kiremt bet ayseram.
You can't build a house for last winter.
—Amharic saying

Contents

Halfway Heaven

ONE

The Twinning

There is an aristocracy to which the sons of Harvard have belonged . . . the aristocracy which excels in manly sports, carries off the honors and prizes of the learned professions, and bears itself with distinction in all fields of intellectual labor and combat; the aristocracy which in peace stands firmest for the public honor and renown, and in war rides first into the murderous thicket.

—Charles W. Eliot, president of Harvard

(1869)

Harvard's commencement is among the most festive in the land. By the first week of June the square of lawn between Widener Library and Memorial Chapel has been reseeded and grown new and green again. A large pastel tent has been erected, as if in preparation for an enormous wedding, and red silk flags are strung all around on trees, bearing the Harvard motto "Veritas" and the insignia of each of the Harvard houses where undergraduates live. World eminences give historic speeches—Mother Teresa, Colin Powell, Václav Havel. The Marshall Plan was announced at the commencement of 1947.

The whole of undergraduate life at Harvard seems to lead toward the moment of graduation. With a ninety-seven percent graduation rate—among the highest in the country—students understand that to attend Harvard is to have the opportunity to graduate from Harvard, and all that that bestows upon one. On one's résumé, at work, on a blind date, it is a fact that connotes not so much intelligence as chosenness—a destiny to do significant, lucrative work, a kind of good luck charm whose spell is always new.

As the seniors are welcomed to the company of educated men and women, their parents clap and cry—it is their *laudes* too. Among the most touching sights are the immigrant parents: gathered around their sons and daughters, the American Dream seems alight in their faces—everything they journeyed to this country for accomplished in a moment.

The speaker for the 1996 commencement—Harvard's three hundred forty-fifth—is Dr. Harold Varmus, director of the National Institutes of Health. He gives an earnest account of his journey from studying literature at Harvard to committing to medicine when he realized the power medicine has to alleviate human suffering. He describes the enormous progress of medicine in his lifetime—the development of the kidney transplant and the cure of polio, the crippling disease of his childhood—and reminds the audience how much there is still to be done. He enjoins the new graduates to enlist in the front lines on the battlefields of science.

There is no reference, in his speech or throughout the long commencement day, to two girls who are not there to graduate with their class, and whose fate reflects a problem that has not disappeared with the progress of medicine: the problem of evil.

O n May 28, 1995, shortly before the previous commencement, Sinedu Tadesse, a twenty-year-old junior from Ethiopia, murdered her roommate, Trang Phuong Ho, an immigrant from Vietnam. The girls had lived together for two years, but during the spring of their junior year Trang had decided not to live with Sinedu again and had chosen new roommates for senior year. During the last week of term, Sinedu sent a photograph of herself and an anonymous typewritten note to the student newspaper. The note said: "Keep this picture. There will soon be a very juicy story involving the person in this picture."

The morning that students were supposed to move out of their residence, Dunster House, for the summer—the Sunday of Memorial Day weekend—Sinedu set her alarm for early in the morning, and then stabbed Trang forty-five times with a knife as she lay sleeping in her bed. Lying beside Trang, sleeping head to toe, was a visiting girlfriend, Thao Nguyen, a recent Vietnamese immigrant who had been staying with her for the weekend. Thao awoke to see her friend being stabbed and tried to grab the knife from Sinedu, but was injured herself and went for help. She ran downstairs, bleeding, into the courtyard, where students called the police, but by the time they came Sinedu had hanged herself in the bathroom, with a noose she had prepared ahead of time, and both girls were dead.

The events were met with stunned bewilderment. "The questions were endless. Could Harvard have intervened? Why did Tadesse snap? Were there unseen warning signs? Why does evil exist?" *Newsweek* asked. "The sense of mystery is unlikely to lift anytime soon," *People* magazine wrote. "Neither Student Complained of Problems," the *Boston Globe* reported. Another *Globe* story quoted a Harvard official: "There is no conventional motive. It is not about sex or revenge. There is no apparent reason." Under the heading "Harvard Deaths Leave a Puzzle Whose Central Piece May Never Be Found," the *New York Times* reported that "interviews with students and faculty members who knew the two women . . . indicate that the key to last weekend's events has thus far eluded everyone."

The media descriptions of Sinedu and Trang invariably made them sound like twins: polite, gentle-mannered, petite, five-feet-tall, hard-working twenty-year-old foreign premed junior biology majors "destined for some of life's highest pinnacles." Under the heading "Two Quiet Students Whose Paths Met," the *New York Times* detailed the twinning: "They certainly seemed well matched. Both had risen from humble circumstances . . . Ms. Tadesse's father had been a political prisoner. At age ten Ms. Ho had escaped from Vietnam on a fishing boat . . . both women dreamed of becoming doctors so they could help others. Both hewed to the family-centered traditions of their homelands, and both were valedictorians of their high school classes."

The deaths were also seen as wrapped in the mythology of Dunster House. Old and beautiful, by the banks of the Charles River, Dunster—one of thirteen upper-class residences—has an aura of gloom, and was connected with two previous suicides that spring. Students in the house recalled having seen the two students always together, taking courses, studying, or eating. As Leslie Dunton-Downer, a junior fellow at the Harvard Society of Fellows and an affiliate of Dunster House, explained: "In the mind of Dunster House Sinedu and Trang had this twinlike co-dependency—this complete linked heterogeneity, living together in one of those dark little embryonic double rooms."

Part of the sense of mystery was owing to the extreme rarity of the crime. Less than nine percent of murders are committed by women and almost all those are mothers killing their children or women killing abusive partners. It was the first murder between two students in the University's history. The last comparable crime at Harvard took place in 1849, when an instructor at Harvard Medical College, John Webster, killed and dismembered a former classmate, George Parkman, hiding the body parts in a school privy—a crime that shocked the Boston Brahmin community.

Sinedu and Trang's deaths presented a puzzle the university would prefer to have forgotten. A few months after the murder a letter to all Harvard parents from Harry R. Lewis, dean of Harvard College, assured parents that both girls had been integrated into Harvard's "carefully woven advising system." The letter concluded: "Although several news articles have speculated on what might have caused Ms. Tadesse to act as she did, it seems unlikely that we will ever have an adequate understanding of the event."

As it happened, the murder/suicide occurred just a month after a scandal when the Harvard admissions committee discovered that an applicant, Gina Grant, had bludgeoned her mother to death with a candlestick five years previously. A great deal of debate ensued: should a murderer be admitted to Harvard? The answer was no, the acceptance withdrawn.

Sinedu, however, was rarely spoken of as a murderer. A peculiar discourse developed on campus in which, rather than being viewed distinctly, as murderer and victim, the girls were recalled in one breath, as if their deaths were the result of some unfathomable blood rite, like a suicide pact, about which no one could say who was to blame or where the evil lay. In a small campus service of "Prayers and Remembrances" in which neither girl was referred to by name, the Reverend Peter Gomes, the university minister, said only, "For all that was good in these girls, Lord bless them; for the forces of evil beyond their control, Lord forgive them. Lord, heal, as well, the rupture the evil has made in our hearts. For words fail us; analysis runs cold."

There was a good deal of discussion on campus about whether there should be a joint scholarship in the name of both girls—a macabre kind of Political Correctness. There was a confused sense that there were two victims; as Diep Nguyen, the co-president of the Vietnamese Students Association and a friend of Trang's, explained, "In some way we don't understand we feel Sinedu is a victim as well—we're not blaming anyone."

"They seemed so similar," a student at Dunster House commented. "Why would anyone kill someone so like herself?"

Sinedu would certainly have been pleased by the confusion. A kindred spirit—a perfect partner to complete and mirror her, like the missing half of Aristophanes' divided egg—was something Sinedu seems to have believed, at one point, she had found in Trang. Through her single act of violence, Sinedu's reality became the ultimate one, linking the two girls through death in a common fate, so that in memory they are bonded in a way in which Trang has no choice, and which in life never existed.

The actual differences between the two girls were evident almost immediately. On June 1, the Thursday after the deaths, Harvard officials held an informational meeting in a large auditorium, organized at the request of students from the Vietnamese Students Association. Tables were stacked with memos announcing funeral arrangements (which Harvard was paying for): shuttle buses would leave the campus at five-thirty that night and take students to Sinedu's wake at the Faggas Funeral Home in Watertown. Visiting hours for Trang Ho were being held at a funeral parlor in Medford, and her funeral was scheduled for Saturday morning.

The auditorium was packed with nearly three hundred and fifty students, faculty, reporters, and cameramen. Reporters from news organizations from CNN to *Hard Copy* had descended upon campus after the murder. No one could recall such a frenzy of media interest before, although the killing was the climax of a year of misfortunes at Harvard. Along with the Gina Grant controversy, there had been three previous suicides, two students were convicted of stealing money from a charity, and Harvard president Neil Rudenstine took a three-month sabbatical owing to nervous exhaustion. In the days since the murder, reporters had been seen scaling the walls of the newly guarded Dunster House. *Inside Edition* offered money to any students willing to appear on the show, others dangled job offers. Many of the media outlets have Harvard alumni staff, who were sent to cover the tragedy. *The New Yorker* offered me an assignment—if I could find anything out.

I had met Sinedu once when I was teaching in the English Department. (I had graduated from Harvard in 1987, where I had lived in Dunster House, and then returned to teach for a year in 1992.) The meeting with Sinedu had been brief, but the brush with the dead girl and the odd sense on campus of a hopeless mystery—a mystery beyond insight or analysis in the midst of a place I knew so well—made me want to explore it.

I had been struck by a news program I had heard on which the commentator said that, a few days before her death, Sinedu Tadesse had tantalized the press by presaging "a juicy story." Yet in the wake of the event, the commentator continued, the questions remained. What is that story? Is it a story about a lonely student at a negligent institution? Or is it a story about an Ethiopian and her personal or cultural or national history? A story of female friendship and a relationship between two women—a story of rejection, envy, or love? Or a story of psychopathology and mental illness?

A silence fell upon the assembled guests: a therapist, a student, a school official. Not only did no one know the real story, no one even had an orientation—a sense of where to search for answers, which doors to knock upon.

The meeting that day is introduced by Betty Cung, one of the leaders of the Harvard Vietnamese Students Association. She explains that the Vietnamese students have invited officials from President Rudenstine's office and the police and the district attorney's office to speak. She also says that Vietnamese students believe that the tragedy is as great for those who knew Sinedu as it is for Trang's friends, so they have asked members of the African Students Association to relay their own memories of Sinedu.

Lieutenant John Rooney of the Harvard police stands and announces that Harvard is fully cooperating with the district attorney's office on the investigation. The dean of students, Archie C. Epps III, expresses the university's desire to help students all it can in the wake of the tragedy. He reads a quotation from a speech President Franklin Roosevelt gave on the Tercentenary celebration of the founding of Harvard, in which he quoted Euripides: "There are many shapes of things, mystery, past hope and fear, a path where no man sought, so hath it fallen here."

Five students from the Vietnamese Students Association read prepared statements about Trang. One describes her devotion to her family—boat people from Vietnam. Her parents were divorced and her mother and sister had arrived in the country only two years previously. She returned home every weekend to the nearby suburb of Medford to help her younger sister with homework, translate English documents for her mother, and do household chores. She worked eighteen hours a week at two jobs to support them financially. She was "a crucial member of her family and their great hope for the future." Another describes how she found time to be vice president of the Vietnamese Students Association, and to tutor refugees in Dorchester, a working-class Boston community. She had given up her desire to return to Vietnam the previous summer in order to work at the Dana-Farber Cancer Institute and to do research for her biology thesis so that she might achieve her dream of becoming a pediatrician. She always used her time productively; she would have felt guilty doing otherwise. "Without a doubt," the last student to speak concludes, "considering her compassionate and cheerful personality, she would have been an outstanding doctor." The establishment of a Trang Ho Family Fund is announced.

Then a representative of the Harvard African Students Association, Adey Fisseha, stands and expresses deepest condolences to Trang Ho's family and friends on behalf of their organization. She says that the African students have no idea what happened but that they wanted to balance things out by presenting a portrait of Sinedu. The word, she says, which best portrayed Sinedu is "nice." Whenever she bumped into Sinedu she always enjoyed talking to her. Inati Ntshanga, the president of the African Students Association, describes Sinedu as a "very responsible student. She was mostly the first person to come to meetings, but also the first to leave because she was a very quiet person." He says he didn't know her well, but she was "very soft-spoken," and "it's a shock and a surprise that this happened."

A break is declared during which it is announced that the rest of the meeting is intended only for members of the Harvard community and the press is requested to leave—with the exception of the Harvard press, the student and university newspapers. It's a uniquely Harvard moment—the ousting of outsiders—and a sense of excited secrecy tightens the audience, as if officials will reveal the mystery to us, the ones who deserve to know. Without thinking, I include myself among them. (My last position, as a tutor, had ended only the previous semester. And I had lived around Harvard all my life; both my parents and brother were educated at Harvard, my father is the Winthrop Professor of History and my mother has taught at Harvard as well.)

But just before the meeting is to reconvene, a woman taps me on my shoulder. "If you're going to write anything about this, you have to *leave,*" she says in a low accusatory voice. I recognize her dimly: she is some kind of administrator. I am aware for the first time that the assignment will place me in a new relation to my alma mater: a member of the press. One of the Vietnamese student organizers of the meeting had explained to me that they had specifically asked for press to be included in the meeting because they *wanted* Harvard student reactions to be on the record—but the administration wants to control what is printed. I glance around and see the reporters from the *Herald* and the *Globe* not moving. I shake my head at her, uneasily, but I can feel her gaze boring into my back as the meeting begins again.

The administration needn't have worried, though; as it turns out, no one says anything particularly surprising. Diep Nguyen says that

Harvard should have set up an informational meeting earlier so that students wouldn't have had to get news of their friends' deaths from the media. Her comment is met with applause. Other students criticize the advising system—voicing feelings of isolation and lack of support. Alex Cho, the head of the Asian Students Association, says he hasn't had contact with his tutor (the graduate student assigned to be his adviser) all year and students applaud again.

Dean Epps moderates the discussion, listening to student complaints and acknowledging them thoughtfully. I remember sitting in his office as an undergraduate, telling him of my own roommate problems and how urgent they had seemed. He says he has received many concerned calls from parents and that a hot line has been set up for them to call. He also says that Harvard has a great many advising resources, but perhaps they could be better utilized. However, he adds, he has never come across a suicide that did not have a very long history, predating college. A woman asks whether the administration would permit a spiritual cleansing in the dorm room where the murder took place.

"What tradition are you representing?" Dean Epps asks.

"Just a general spiritual tradition," she says.

He shakes his head no, but everyone in the room seems struck by the question. Someone asks how the girls were paired together and a woman who identifies herself as Carol Finn, the assistant to the Dunster House master, stands up and says that she does not recall anything about the rooming arrangement. Her voice is strident, defending herself against responsibility for the unlucky coupling. She refers to them as "girls," as everyone does. (I wonder whether it is because they are portrayed as innocent, virginal foreigners—without boyfriends—or simply because they are dead?)

The meeting breaks up and people cluster in the hall. Members of the press swarm around groups of students. I see a former student of mine, Elie Kaunfer, who tells me he has been hired by the *New York Times* as a stringer to research the story.

"It's a hard story to report," he says. "Sinedu didn't have any friends."

"Maybe she has close friends who didn't talk at the meeting," I say.

He shrugs. "No one's been able to find them," he says.

At five-thirty that night two red and white mini-buses line up at the edge of Harvard Yard to convey people to Sinedu's wake. A peculiar sense comes over me, climbing into the bus I took as a student back and forth from Harvard Yard to Dunster House by the river. Students are sitting, looking down at their feet, sober and uncomfortable; no one talks or cries. They are awkwardly dressed, the guys in jeans and ties, the young women in skirts with backpacks. When I was an undergraduate, my best friend, Bibi Lee, a junior at the University of California at Berkeley, was killed by her boyfriend while they were running in a park outside San Francisco. I remember riffling frantically through my wardrobe the morning of her funeral, weeping into my only black dress, which was short and sequined.

The Faggas Funeral Home in Watertown has the depressing look of a low-rent accountant's office. There are several dozen Ethiopians and a few Harvard officials, including President Rudenstine, in a dark suit, looking cloaked in his own thoughts. I had heard Sinedu had relatives in Boston, but it is hard to tell which they are. Two heavy-robed priests chant in what I assume is Amharic, but later found out was Ge'ez, the ancient language of Ethiopia, in which the liturgy of the Ethiopian Orthdox Church is conducted. The room is dominated by the casket where Sinedu lies, garbed in a high-necked white satin dress, like a cheap wedding gown.

An Ethiopian woman begins to scream, her wails mingling with the priests' chants—a screaming which continues, disembodied, frightening, in the stifling summer air. I close my eyes against the sound and find myself repeating over and over: "Lord bless us and keep us, Lord cause his face to shine down upon us"—a prayer I didn't even know I knew—don't even know whether it is Jewish or Christian. The Ethiopian woman stands and faints. A crowd of people gather around her; President Rudenstine kneels beside her.

The service ends and people file past the coffin. The body is being shipped for burial to Ethiopia the next day, I have heard. I have never seen an open casket before. Throughout the service I had been reluctant to look at Sinedu—as if her face would contain the violence that had brought her here. But her face, I see now, is waxy, bloated from the effects of strangulation and utterly empty. Whatever had compelled her to take life—her own and another girl's—is gone. Bibi was buried in a closed cedar casket because by the time her body was found it had decayed beyond recognition. Afterward I was haunted by a tiny grain of doubt that there had somehow been a mistake and she hadn't really been in there—a hope that took years and years to ebb away. I think how, if I had seen her like this at first, I would have understood all along that she was dead and what that meant: how the spirit flees.

People head toward the door. There is no visitors' book to sign, no one to offer condolences to. None of the Ethiopians identify themselves as family or speak to the students. We step outside, where darkness has fallen. The bus ride back to campus is silent.

At home, I take aspirin and get into bed. I stare at my blank notebook and write nothing.

A student in the African Students Association gives me the phone number of Sinedu's cousins in Brookline, who had arranged the wake and had been dealing with the police. At the moment I am given the number, it seems like a break, but when I get home I realize I will have to call them now—these strangers in grief who must be dealing with so many things they never wanted or prepared for. It occurs to me one of the main things that reporters do is call people who don't want to hear from them: an idea that I hate. I sometimes sound so shy calling people I do know that they mistake me for a small child.

I decide to contact the victim's family and friends instead. I call Betty Cung, one of the leaders of the Harvard Vietnamese Students Association (HVA), and arrange to meet with a group of students. She sounds exhausted and drained: the Vietnamese students have spent all week arranging for the big meeting and the funeral, setting up a fund for the family, the Trang Ho Family Fund. Their own families are arriving for commencement, when they will have to go through the planned festivities. "Senior week," the week before commencement, is supposed to be devoted to partying—the "Booze Cruise," senior barbecue, graduation ball: a time of giddy anticipation and ordinary loss, terribly transformed for them now into a different kind of farewell.

The day before commencement, I meet with four students at an outdoor café. It is a chilly overcast morning; we huddle at an outdoor wrought-iron table, holding cups of milky coffee. "HVA is like a family," Diep Nguyen, a close friend of Trang's, says. "That's what Trang worked to make it like." They tell me that in Trang's role as vice-president she often made a hundred phone calls trying to get people to come to an event. I'm struck by this detail: from the press accounts, I had had the impression both girls had been socially reclusive.

Everyone recalls the warm gestures Trang was always making—cards she gave them to encourage them with an exam or at a special time. Deanna Nguyen recalls how Trang gave her a stuffed bear for Valentine's Day with a card saying how she valued their friendship; she can't remember a female friend having done something like that before. She has that bear now, she says, and it's so valuable to her. "When someone dies you always portray the victim as so perfect and good," she says passionately, "but with Trang it's really true—she really was that perfect—she really shone as a person."

"I still can't believe she's in the grave," Diep says. "She worked so hard and never had the chance to reap the benefits."

Hans Stohrer, who is not Vietnamese but socializes with the other students, tells me that he is going to medical school in the fall. "I guess I'll be realizing Trang's dream," he says. "She inspired a lot of us. I know how hard she worked." He had met Trang at MICAS, a tutoring program for Vietnamese refugees in which they had all volunteered at one point.

"Community work is a Vietnamese tradition," Diep explains. "We're all involved in helping new refugees."

Another friend, Khoi Luu, with whom I meet later, taught reading and health and sex education with Trang at MICAS the previous summer. He remembers how they would do gender-role workshops in which Trang would ask the student whether the woman should do all the housework and the students would yell, "Yes!" and Trang would yell, "No!"

"She was always really nice, but her students knew she wouldn't take any shit," Khoi said. "She saw younger versions of herself in them. She wanted to encourage them to rise and not join gangs. She was very committed—it was a three-hour round trip to Dorchester by public transportation every day.

"She was spunky," Khoi says. "She liked to sing a lot. She had a bad voice, and we'd always tease her." He remembers how at a HVA fund-raising dance, where the women had to "buy" the men, he had pointed out his friend Dat, who had not been bought, and even though Trang and Dat had never gotten along that well, she paid twenty dollars and danced with him. Now HVA is donating the profits of that dance to Trang's family, he says, so part of that is Trang's money now.

Trang's friends find it difficult to remember much about Trang's relationship with Sinedu. "Trang had many best friends," Hans Stohrer says, "but even when things were good between them, Sinedu was never one of them." Trang's closest friend was Thao Nguyen whom Trang had also met at MICAS and who had been sleeping over the night Trang was killed. Trang and Sinedu had been friendly the first year, but by the end of sophomore year things had cooled, and it was Hans's impression that Trang had agreed to room with Sinedu a second year for convenience more than affection—and then the relationship had deteriorated. Trang had never talked much about it, other than to complain that Sinedu was too messy—even to the point of leaving fruit in the room to rot and attract flies.

"She didn't say much about it. I urged her talk to Sinedu to try to work it out. But she wasn't really interested in doing that. I don't think Sinedu was that important to her."

"But Trang must have been very important to Sinedu," I say.

"We hear people saying they must have been lovers," Hans says. It's an obvious thought: one does not ordinarily associate friendship with the degree of passion necessary to create forty-five stab wounds. Something of great importance had clearly been at stake.

Hans says he is pretty sure that a lesbian relationship was not a possibility. He says that he and Trang had what he described as a romantic friendship—although one they both pulled back from. He remembers Trang having had crushes on boys, but "she wasn't at a point in her life where she wanted to be that emotionally dependent on one person," Hans says. "She wanted to focus on her family and her studies."

Members of the African Students Association all tell me that they didn't know Sinedu that well, and they don't know anyone who did. They are worried about how Sinedu reflects on African students—that the incident will fuel racism and reinforce the stereotype of Asians as the "good minority" and blacks as the bad, destructive one. Students mention a 1991 murder at Dartmouth College in which an Ethiopian national, Haile Selassie Girmay, had hacked two Ethiopian physics graduate student roommates to death because one of them had rejected his marriage proposal. He pleaded insanity—his attorney arguing that his instability came out of the turmoil of his childhood homeland—but he was convicted of first-degree murder.

An article in *Boston* magazine described the Dunster House murder as a blow to Harvard's vision of itself as a multicultural domain, quoting former Harvard historian Simon Schama as saying: "The fact that this tragedy involved two third world students adds something very awful to Harvard's sense of itself as a melting pot."

Students who knew her do not recall Sinedu as troubled, particularly lonely, or unusual in any way. Ashwini Sukthankar recalls Sinedu as "quiet, mousy-looking, intensely private, not desperate or longing to reach out." She says that she and other friends as well feel that Sinedu was "not crying for help. One had the feeling that making any kind of contact was too much of a strain for her. She might have seemed a little lonely, but not in a way that was reaching out to people. A lot of students used the African Students Association as a nexus for dating, but Sinedu showed no interest in any of that." When I ask whether Sinedu could have had a romantic attachment to Trang, Ashwini says she finds it hard to imagine Sinedu as a sexual person at all. "If she was a lesbian," she says, "I doubt she was even out to herself."

Like all foreign students, Sinedu had been assigned to a host family—who it turned out was the family of the director of the Harvard-Radcliffe Parents Association, Ellen Hatfield Towne. I call her several times, but she returns the call to the Harvard news office—the office in charge of press control—which relays the message that she doesn't want to talk.

The only close friend of Sinedu's that anyone recalls is Nebiyeleul (Neb) Tilahun, a fellow Ethiopian from Sinedu's high school who had come to Harvard with her. But he had gone home to Ethiopia for the summer immediately after the murder without speaking to anyone.

When I finally make the call to Sinedu's cousin in Brookline, he tells me to leave them alone and slams down the phone. I stand for a moment, holding the phone, wishing I wasn't taking the rejection so personally. I remind myself that I'm doing what I'm supposed to, by calling them, and they're doing what they should, by protecting themselves, in the dance in which reporters always engage. I send a note, and then a week goes by without a response, so I send a second note and, to my surprise, he calls me and agrees to meet.

He is waiting when I arrive at the café. He asks me not to print his name, and even though it has been in the press in every story about the murder, I agree. He tells me that he and his wife emigrated from Ethiopia fifteen years previously and that he is a businessman, but declines to specify what his business is. He has also brought a tape recorder and asks to tape the conversation.

In an interview the *Boston Globe* conducted with Sinedu's cousin, his wife, Sinedu's older brother Seiffe, and several other relatives shortly after the murders, Sinedu is described as a calm, cheerful, outgoing student who had a large family network in the Boston area, adapted easily to life at Harvard, and was not shy about discussing problems. "Sinedu has been portrayed as a quiet loner who suffered from culture shock . . . several of her relatives . . . say the prevailing portrait is '100 percent wrong,' " the article reads, " 'Sinedu loved life,' her cousin said. 'This is completely out of her character.' "

But by the time of our meeting Sinedu's cousin doesn't bother with any of that. He tells me that at first he and his wife did not believe that Sinedu could have committed murder. But after many conversations with the police, he says that he has been persuaded, although his wife still has doubts. The reason he decided to meet with me, he says, is that he wants to understand what happened. What do I think?

I don't know, I say: I want to know what he thinks.

A stalemate sets in; he eyes me suspiciously. It becomes clear to me why he has agreed to meet me and why he is recording the conversation; he had imagined *I* would be able to explain things to him. I stress how little I know and ask about her family in Ethiopia. He tells me he doesn't know them well. He and his wife met Sinedu for the first time when she came to America her freshman year. But he never got to know her, he adds; she lived in their house for two summers and several holidays, but she never opened up to him—she would never even accept a beer from him. She seemed most comfortable playing with their children. He concludes that she must have had some deep problem she never told anyone about, which now no one will ever know.

He recalls the Sunday they were supposed to pick her up at school to move her out for the summer. It was a perfect end of a May day, the gates of Dunster House flung open, the gilded dome—modeled after Christ Church in Oxford—glinting in the sun, high above the blue river. Instead, they had to go identify the body at the morgue—an evil-smelling underground place. He kept looking at Sinedu's hands. They looked so small. Over and over he thought: How could those hands have done such a thing?

S inedu had come to see me once, when she was a freshman, in the crowded first few days of the 1992 spring term. I had spent the preceding few days reading a hundred applications in order to choose a dozen students for a seminar on autobiographical writing I was teaching in the English Department. The list of successful applicants had been posted on the door. It was an unfortunate system—that in order to take a writing class to learn you had to prove you were already accomplished—but it was the way many things were done at Harvard.

I remember my own anxiety as an undergraduate applying to creative writing courses, reassuring myself I had published poetry to submit with my application. But I remember the shock I had felt whenever I tried to explore something new at college, only to discover it was necessary to compete with students who were already well versed—to take comparative literature courses with students who had gone to boarding school in Paris or Milan. Even extracurricular activities were competitive. In order to join the *Advocate*—

a literary magazine that had published the early work of e. e. cummings, T. S. Eliot, and Norman Mailer—one had to demonstrate sufficient command of contemporary letters by writing mock reviews of poetry or fiction for six weeks, and then undergoing an interview by a board of peers.

There was a light knock on the door and Sinedu came in. She was small with large, heavy-lidded eyes and an air of nervous decorum. "I saw my name wasn't on the list," she told me. I tried to recall her writing sample: it had made no impression. In addition, upper classmen had priority in applying to the class.

"In Ethiopia where I come from I have seen terrible violence and poverty and things no one would understand," she told me, leaning forward slightly, her voice low and self-dramatizing. Another rich Harvard student from the third world, I decided impatiently: they speak of the suffering of their countrymen and turn out to be royalty. I told her to apply again another year. She rose to go.

"You could write something and send it to me. I'm always happy to read students' work," I called guiltily after her. She never would, I knew, and I'd never follow up. I'd be busy with the students I had chosen.

Eighteen months later, I was spending a long weekend in a small town in New Hampshire when my mother called to tell me something terrible had happened: a Harvard student—a Dunster House student—had killed her roommate and both girls were now dead. "You didn't know them, did you?" she asked.

"No," I said. "Why would I?" Later I went and got the newspapers and stared at the picture of Sinedu, recognition slowly dawning.

In the days that followed, the significance of the coincidence grew in my mind as I rethought the brief encounter again and again, trying to recall the forgotten nuances of her words. Sinedu was a premedical biology major; her transcript showed nothing more than required humanities courses. No one I spoke to remembered her having been interested in creative writing. Why had she come to me? What had she wanted to express that had made her so eager to take the class? How intimately I would have known her—as I knew my other students—had I admitted her to the class! Why hadn't I? I made exceptions to rules all the time; my classes were filled with extra students. I had felt a slight sense of relief when she left the office. I was one in a long line of people—as it turned out—whom Sinedu had reached out to and who did not respond to her. I had missed my chance to be her writing teacher—to help her tell her own stories. But she left behind a story, dark and cryptic—one I wanted to decipher.

I would have to go to Ethiopia, I realized. There was no one in America who knew her.

TWO

Sinedu

Ethiopia, often called the cradle of civilization because the ancestors of Homo sapiens originated there four million years ago, has a terrible modern history—marked by poverty, war, and political repression. On the plane to Ethiopia, I skim through a pile of books about the country—histories that read with a kind of fairy-tale grimness.

In the time of Christ, Ethiopia had been the powerful kingdom of Abyssinia, a thriving Red Sea trading empire, mentioned in the Bible and Greek literature, often as a metaphor for remoteness. But having lost its northern province in the Eritrean independence war, it lies landlocked now in the horn of Africa in a cluster of some of the other poorest countries in Africa: Somalia, the Sudan, Chad, Eritrea, Niger, Zaire.

During the more than half-century reign of Emperor Haile Selassie most Ethiopians lived as peasants in rural poverty under a feudal arrangement, leasing land from a few big landowners, such as the Church. In 1974 the Derg, a council of military officers, overthrew the emperor and began a massive communist revolution, nationalizing everything under the auspices of the Workers' Party of Ethiopia. The revolution swiftly turned to bloodletting, and large numbers of people were imprisoned, tortured, and executed. Many of the country's scant resources were used in futile wars with Somalia and the Eritrean secessionists. After nearly two decades of rule, the Derg was defeated in 1991 by the Ethiopian People's Revolutionary Democratic Front—Tigrayan rebels from the north.

The new government was left with a country in ruins. There is no industry in Ethiopia; the only real export products are hides, coffee, and qat leaves, which release an amphetamine when chewed. The economy is based entirely on agriculture and herding. The land has been depleted by continuous cultivation for the last five thousand years, and the population has increased steadily, so that each generation inherits a smaller and less rich plot of ground. In times of drought, the country starves.

Ethiopia's main problems are generally described as twofold: a lack of natural resources, and the warring tribal divisions of its people. There are eighty different ethnic groups, speaking at least sixty-four different languages, in a country about twice the size of Texas. The prognosis for the future is bleak: while food production declines each year, the population relentlessly increases (the average woman bears more than seven children) so that more and more people are expected to be hungry.

The statistics of Ethiopian poverty seem almost fantastical. Sixty percent of the population lives in absolute poverty: malnourished, without access to health services or safe drinking water. Life expectancy is only fifty years. Ten thousand women die in childbirth every year. A fifth of children—half a million—under the age of five die every year. Two thirds of the surviving children are physically and mentally stunted by malnutrition.

On the plane with me are a group of Americans from U.S. AID and another aid organization. Aid to Ethiopia, which had been cut off during the communist regime, has now been restored. The aid workers tell me that they are afraid that, rather than increasing with the rising need, aid will be further cut by the Republican Congress. Although in total dollars America is a large foreign aid donor, in terms of the percentage of our gross national product we actually rank last among the twenty-one industrialized donor nations. The Japanese, the Germans, the French, the Irish—all contribute much larger percentages of their wealth to foreign aid. I puzzle about this: why are they more generous than we?

The aid workers tell me about an interesting survey which canvasses people on their views of foreign aid.[1] Most people guess that the United States spends about a fifth of its budget on foreign aid, which they consider excessive. In fact, though, after a steady decline over the past two decades, less than one percent of the budget is appropriated for foreign aid, and the largest share of that goes to military aid. Although most people say that they think five percent is an appropriate figure—five times what is actually spent—the aid workers are afraid further cuts will be forthcoming.

The aid workers have the cheery straightforwardness of people who do good work—the sort of work that is easy to justify. I blush slightly when they ask what I am doing. They are going to provide aid to the country, to give balm to its wounds, and I am going to probe them—possibly even do further damage.

I did not call Sinedu's family before I left to tell them I was coming. I had read an article in the *New York Times* in which Sinedu's father stated that as a child Sinedu was never angry, never lost her temper, was never depressed, and always won the highest possible grades: " 'This is why it is very difficult to swallow that Sinedu committed murder and suicide,' Mr. Tadesse said, weeping. 'Impossible.' "

The idea that he had wept had stopped me short. Would he weep if I called him? I realize it is ridiculous now—traveling halfway around the world without knowing whether the family will talk to me, or even whether they are in Addis Ababa this week—but here I am, on an eighteen-hour flight, the word "weeping" dissolving into uneasy dreams.

Surrounded by a vast expanse of lawn and tropical gardens, where goats graze ravenously, the Hilton Hotel rises like a fortress, a huge concrete structure built, as if by giants, on an entirely different scale than the rest of the city. Through the fence on one side of the grounds a slum is visible—clusters of mud huts with little tin roofs—where, perhaps, the owners of the goats live. The driver unloads my luggage; I hand him a twenty-dollar bill and he drops to his knees and kisses my hand. The average worker in Ethiopia earns only a hundred and twenty dollars a year. "Pretty soon," the other passenger, a German diplomat, tells me, "you'll be bargaining over pennies."

That night I stand on the balcony of my room, overlooking the city. The steam from the outdoor swimming pool just below me rises into the fragrant air. Beyond, the lights of the city look small and scattered as a candlelight vigil. The words of Czech President Havel's Harvard commencement speech, given a week after the murder, float into my mind. "I have not lost hope," he said, "because I am persuaded again and again that, lying dormant in the deepest roots of most, if not all, cultures, there is an essential similarity. . . ."

Nothing in the Hilton quite works like an ordinary hotel. In the small tourist office in the lobby, the next morning, six employees are sitting around, idly chatting. When I ask where their tours go, they respond agreeably, "Anywhere you like." I inquire about a brochure, and they say they don't have any, but they are thinking of getting some printed. I ask about a map of the city and they confer with one another and then point to the wall, where a map of the entire country is pinned up. I locate Addis Ababa on it, but it is small and crudely drawn, like an illustration in a children's book. The hotel elevator doesn't line up with the floor; the detail strikes me—the small misalignment, the gap that will not close. I mention it to a hotel clerk and he shrugs—they don't know how to fix it. Conversation is difficult; the employees have learned English from native Ethiopians.

America is generally organized to make information available; Ethiopia's disorganization is compounded by a sense of secrecy. I had come with the names of a few contacts, but when I'm able to get a phone line, I find it impossible to ascertain whether I have the right number; even when the voice on the other end of the line speaks English, they refuse to say whether they know the person I'm seeking.

An American staying at the hotel who works at the American embassy, arranging visas, tells me that one of the most striking things he has noticed in his job is how much Ethiopians suffer during interviews. They hate answering questions about themselves; they are frightened the information will be used against them—as it had been during the Derg regime.

I try calling the Amharic paper, but no one will speak to me there so I call the English-language newspaper. A woman there tells me the paper had been aware of the tragedy, but they were unable to find out anything about it so they simply reprinted a small article from the AP wire service.

"Unable," I repeat, my heart sinking. "Why didn't you interview the family?"

"We didn't want to disturb them," she says sharply.

At the other English-language paper, I talk to a British woman who explains to me that there is no tradition of investigative journalism in Ethiopia. Under the Derg, newspapers functioned primarily as press releases for the government; news was the government building a new bridge, not a private citizen committing a crime. The papers are trying to become more independent now, but they still have to be very careful. The woman explains that her boss at the paper had been called in for questioning recently to account for an article; he was held in jail for three days and it was very frightening for them all.

———

On the streets of Addis Ababa, the statistic *the third poorest country in the world* takes on visual meaning. The old-fashioned phrase "third world" comes to mind—as if removed from the world with which I am familiar not merely by geography but also by time. The city looks as I have imagined the slums of previous centuries. The streets smell of livestock and open sewers. Although it is the middle of the day, everywhere there are people. Most adults are unemployed and most children don't go to school and houses are too small—without windows or electricity—to stay inside. Malnourished children, garbed in donated American clothing, try to sell shoestrings or Kleenex or simply hold out their hands to beg in the mud of the rainy season. Coffins are stacked up for sale by the side of the road next to stands selling fruit. The small coffins are stacked on top—the ones for children.

Past a leper colony, the low red gates of International Community School (ICS) open to a compound of pretty, airy buildings. The school is closed for the summer, but some teachers and secretaries are still there. They greet me with exclamations of sorrow and incredulity.

News of the deaths had reached the school slowly. A student had heard of the crime on CNN at the health club in the Hilton Hotel—the only health club in the country—to which the rich locals belong. The day that they found out, the day's lessons were canceled and teachers and students spent the day crying and talking. The school sent flowers and a card to Sinedu's family. Many of the younger students had looked up to Sinedu, the valedictorian of her class. "We talked a lot about what it was like to go to school in the States," Astrid Shiferaw, her chemistry teacher, said. "What could have happened there to make her change this way? The whole hope of the school is to be able to send a student to America."

The small school, designed for the children of foreigners—diplomats, foreign businessmen, and aid workers—gives scholarships to a select few Ethiopians each year, as part of the agreement the school had made with the Derg regime. (The tuition for ICS is $7,500 U.S. dollars a year—an unimaginable sum even for affluent Ethiopians.)

Several of Sinedu's teachers were familiar with her family history. Sinedu's family were Amharas from Menz, the inner circle of Amharas, the ethnic group from which the ruling class was drawn under Emperor Haile Selassie. Sinedu's father, Tadesse Zelleke (Ethiopian children take the father's first name as their last), had been the headmaster of several government schools, and himself had been educated at the American University in Beirut.

Shortly before Sinedu was born, the Derg came to power and the family lost their status. When Sinedu was two, the Red Terror began—a time in which thirty thousand people were killed and massive numbers of others disappeared and were tortured and imprisoned, especially the educated elite. Corpses were dragged to their families' doorsteps in the morning; the soldiers would force the families to pay for the bullet before relinquishing the bodies. When Sinedu was seven and a half, her father was imprisoned without trial for two years on suspicion of rebel sentiments. His cell adjoined that of Negash Kebede, Sinedu's physics teacher. Neither of them had any idea what their fates would be. Sinedu's mother, Atsede, worked as a nurse in a government hospital to keep the family alive. The year he was released half a million Ethiopians died of famine.

While her father was imprisoned, Sinedu continued to attend a Catholic elementary girls' school, reminiscent of nineteenth-century British schools with its neat uniforms and emphasis on memorization, obedience, and churchgoing. She was lucky to be there—in public schools, students sit on dirt floors, a hundred to a class, without books or supplies, for a half day of school—a morning or an afternoon shift. Ethiopia has one of the lowest literacy rates in the world; the average

Ethiopian has only one year of schooling. Only a fifth of children are enrolled in primary schools; less than a tenth go on to high school.

In eighth grade the best students from sixty different elementary schools are chosen to take an exam in English to compete for entrance to ICS. Neb Tilahun—who later went to Harvard with Sinedu—scored the highest in the country; Sinedu the second highest. Then they underwent a round of interviews. "Ability was not enough," Negash Kebede says. "They also had to be fit to enter into an international situation. The interview was about their character, as well as academic capabilities. Sinedu was admitted by unanimous decision. She was a model in character and she did very neat work."

In ninth grade the scholarship students are introduced to the other students—many of whom have attended ICS since kindergarten—at a special inaugural assembly. "It's a strange experience for them," Christopher Cox, a former music teacher, explains. "There is this sense of 'Oh, you native Ethiopian, you've made it now—you've come up to our level. Congratulations.' "

Sinedu distinguished herself academically throughout high school, becoming one of only two students in her class of thirty-two to achieve the prestigious international baccalaureate diploma. She scored the second best in the country in her SATs after Neb Tilahun. She applied and was accepted to twenty-four American colleges, including a full scholarship to the world's richest, most famous university. She would return home a doctor in a country which currently has one doctor for every thirty-five thousand people. The day she got into Harvard, she told people, was the happiest day of her life. She was seventeen years old and she had never been out of the country before.

Teachers cannot imagine the sequence of events that led to their star pupil returning to the country in a coffin. "It is impossible," Yeshi Tekleab, a primary school teacher who knew Sinedu, says. "I did not believe it when I heard it, and when I read there were forty-five stab wounds I knew it was not true. Forty-five. I tried it with a piece of meat and it was impossible. My arms were too tired. I had to give up."

I suggest that I would like to see Sinedu's file, although the current principal of ICS, Dr. Ronald Schultz, had told me on the phone before I came that Sinedu's records were confidential, just as they were at Harvard. But the teachers at ICS that day are sufficiently eager to prove there was nothing wrong with Sinedu that they thrust the file into my hands.

Opening the file, I half expect it to contain some revelation. I remember, as an undergraduate, being in the Dunster House office where my file was kept, and an administrator telling me I had a right to look at it. I hesitated, and then decided not to—as if it might reveal some truth about myself I shouldn't know.

Sinedu's high school principal, Thomas Schindele, wrote:

Sinedu is an extremely dependable person: once committed she can always be counted on to devote herself to a task and complete it.

Her English teacher, Maura McMillin:

Sinedu Tadesse is a conscientious and caring student. Sinedu is a dedicated student with enormous potential for academic and intellectual and social growth. She is mature and wise beyond her years and widely respected for her sensitivity, initiative and insight.

Her math teacher, Laurie Stimson:

It is rare that one meets a grade twelve student who is as self-assured yet as unassuming as Sinedu Tadesse. Sinedu possesses a type of inner peace that shows itself in all her dealings with others. She appears to have glided through the turbulent teenage years and emerged as a confident mature young woman. At ICS she has inadvertently been a pillar of support for many fellow students throughout the years. During the final weeks of the revolution in Ethiopia last spring when tensions were mounting and many expatriates were evacuating, Sinedu's calm and rational attitude towards the situation helped maintain some semblance of order and peace at ICS.

In her studies, Sinedu is highly motivated and diligent. She is well established within the social life of ICS. The other students value her responsible nature and level-headedness and have elected her as their student council secretary and newspaper co-editor. Her leadership abilities have been put to good use in a founding of the French club and in work on the yearbook and carnival committee.

In conclusion, Sinedu is a mature, independent student with varied interests who will adjust well to life at an American University and will invariably leave a lasting impression with the people she meets at the University.

The only recommendation to include a critical note is that of the headmistress of Sinedu's elementary school:

Her participation is remarkable in the sense that she has the ability to organize, encourage and draw out the best from her companions. However, I have also discovered that Sinedu lacks courage to uphold the principles she believes in due to fear of the consequences. She is inclined to feel hurt easily, but with proper guidance, these drawbacks can be corrected when she gets older.

I wish Sinedu a bright future wherever she goes.

"You see," Sinedu's physics teacher, Negash Kebede, tells me, "the data we have just doesn't add up—it is impossible. The only way I could conceive of Sinedu having done this is if she had some problem in her brain like a brain tumor or some hormone imbalance. Here was a person who had a vision of the future and it was very bright and very promising, and she was motivated to work hard and earn that vision. Why would that person want to die? People who commit suicide don't have a vision. I do get awake at nights, thinking about that. How did she lose her vision?"

However, Sinedu's American English teacher, Maura McMillin, while admiring her academic discipline, had a sense all along of Sinedu's personal deficits. She recalls Sinedu as "very composed, very driven. She always had a mission—every decision, every action had a purpose later on. She was not like other students. She was resourceful, meticulous, poised, mature, never goofy or silly—I never remember her laughing or goofing off or attending to her personal happiness. I think it would have gotten in her way."

When asked whether she had liked Sinedu, she says, "She was one of those little academic machines—academically focused to the point of tunnel vision. Her papers were methodical, played it safe, never delved." But this is characteristic of the Ethiopian female scholarship students, she says. She tries to start training them to use the first person in the ninth grade because self-expression is so foreign to them. When Ms. McMillin started teaching at ICS she had to realize that it would be culturally biased to grade Ethiopian students on class participation because girls like Sinedu never felt comfortable expressing themselves in class.

Ms. McMillin's husband, Terefe Kerse, who had been Sinedu's gym teacher, describes her as having been "a typical Ethiopian female, what ninety-five percent of Ethiopian parents want their daughters to be: not verbally opinionated, modest in clothing, gestures, behaviors and tone of voice, courteous, demure, doesn't stand out in a crowd, follows rules, asks no questions." She would never wear gym shorts in gym, he says, for fear of immodesty. He tells me about an Amharic saying: Beware of stagnant waters and calm people.

Neither of them can imagine Sinedu's problem at Harvard was work-related: she had handled so much academic pressure at ICS—she had studied without electricity during the war. "It must have been a betrayal by her friend," Ms. McMillin says. "The friend of hers, her roommate, must have meant a great deal to her."

T he two epigrams Sinedu chose for her high school yearbook are, "Fara! what will be will be," and, "Friendship is life's most precious treasure." But it was a treasure Sinedu seems never to have had. The children of Americans and wealthy Europeans, the other students led a Western-style social life. Ms. McMillin recalls Neb Tilahun—a charismatic student who moved easily between groups of people, integrating quickly, while Sinedu kept largely to herself.

Teachers recall her as a serious, plain-looking girl who shared a car with other students to and from school each day, passing through the streets where government soldiers were forcibly conscripting young men to fight the rebels in Eritrea. Astrid Shiferaw, her chemistry teacher, recalls Sinedu as having one girlfriend, a diplomat's daughter named Lillian, whose family was evacuated to Kenya when the rebels invaded. She remembers Sinedu's desolation when her friend left.

"She didn't seem to want friends," her guidance counselor, Patrick Dyer—a Massachusetts native—says. He saw her as "shy and retiring, incapable of individual expression." He says she moved "deliberately, never spontaneously, but suppression of personal emotions is part of the culture here. There's a shyness, a secrecy collectively in the culture. Intervention into the family is impossible. Ethiopians don't talk to outsiders—they might consult with an elder in their family There is no psychological culture. Most people are so concerned with physical survival that there is no room for other things." He never met Sinedu's parents at any school function, but this was also characteristic of the Ethiopian students.

He recalls Sinedu's whole school career as "a quest for perfection." She took her SATs over and over. "As a guidance counselor, I would tell her, 'You're probably not going to improve your scores that much,' but she did—up to 630 verbal and 770 in math." The detail Mr. Dyer found most striking about Sinedu's death is that the day before the murder/suicide she had skipped her final exam. It was the detail that made him know she had undergone a profound change: "The Sinedu I knew *never* would have missed an exam—she'd be the first at an exam. She was just a quiet young lady with a monumental task in front of her. You couldn't tell her that academics weren't everything because they were. They were her ticket out. Ethiopia is a country with one bad university, where you have no choice what you study, you're herded into medicine or law or whatever the government needs. Admission is based solely on examinations—there is no

American process of recommendations, extracurricular activities, and so on.

"Violence was not foreign to her," he says. "Sinedu was born into the bloodiest time in Ethiopian history—a time when there were bodies on the streets. Every family was touched by the Derg—every family had a member who had violence done to them. On our staff at ICS there are six male teachers. Every single one of them had been jailed during the Derg. There was a girl at school who had a withered arm from being shot. As violent as Sinedu's stabbing was, it might not be that violent in her frame of reference.

"There is lots of tribal hatred and revenge killings in Ethiopia," he says, "although of course they're done by men, not women. Sinedu must have had no practice dealing with her emotions, and therefore she dealt with them in a primitive way. Sometimes, I suppose, you escape your troubles," he says, "and sometimes I suppose you bring them with you."

"No one talks about what happened under the Derg," Maura McMillin says. "The whole thing is very censored. No art or literature or drama has been created out of the violence—no one knows how to process it—no one tells their children what happened to them." Her husband, Terefe Kerse, agrees. (He had been active in the resistance, and was imprisoned and tortured and was awaiting death, but was released unexpectedly in order to play soccer for the country.) Maura tells a story about two Ethiopian women who had emigrated to Atlanta and, by chance, met their torturer—another immigrant—and decided to sue him. "Apparently one of the hardest things about the process for them was simply having to tell their families exactly what had happened to them," she says.

But what violence Sinedu actually experienced, none of them know. "Her family suffered under the Derg," Negash Kebede said, "but every family suffered. There was no unusual suffering."

———

On the way back from the school, I stop at the archeological museum to see Lucy (whom Ethiopians call *Dinqenesh,* meaning "You are amazing")—the skeleton of the oldest woman in the world. Although it is early afternoon, the building is closed and I have to bribe a guard to let me in. There's little to see of Lucy, though, it turns out. She is just a collection of bone fragments arranged on sand in a dirty glass case. I try to picture her, as in a grade school video: a small upright ape, running through the jungle, the pieces of her bones all working together in the service of a thinking, feeling life spirit. How much imagination it would take to try to reconstruct the life which was lived here, I think: how small the clues that remain.

A few days later I meet Neb Tilahun in the pizza parlor of the Hilton Hotel. I had written him care of the registrar's office at Harvard, dubious they would actually forward it, but they did, and it arrived, as it turned out, at a fortuitous moment: after the shock of grief, when he was avoiding reporters and now that he has had some weeks alone in contemplation.

I always have some naive sense of wonder about how reporting works: how can an outsider uncover the inner life of someone she didn't know—someone who had died, and whose death is cloaked in secrecy? Sitting across from Neb, I remember why: people want to tell you. I've always loved the story of King Midas having ass's ears: how his barber had to dig a hole in the earth in which to whisper the secret, he wanted to tell it so badly. Interviewing can work like psychotherapy: people are reluctant and afraid and conscious of the perils of confession, but they want you to evade their defenses and talk them out of their reluctance so they can tell you what they know. Although Neb feels protective of Sinedu as a friend, another student from ICS and an Ethiopian, his strongest desire seems to be to remember Sinedu as clearly as he can and try to figure out what happened—a purpose in which we are aligned and can collaborate.

"I find it very difficult to analyze the situation with what I know of Sinedu," he says. "She was the person I felt most comfortable with at Harvard, a very sincere and cordial person." He had thought he knew everything about her, including her college ID number. At first he did not believe she could have committed a violent crime, but the police persuaded him of the facts, just as they had Sinedu's cousin.

I ask him what her favorite books or movies were, but the question feels wrong to him. "She didn't attach herself to particular things like that," he says. "She knew what she had to do and she did it." She was "dignified and reserved, not the type to go into the dining hall and randomly socialize. I assume she would find that trivial." At home she had had no need to socialize because "her family was strict and she was a superior student and that was the basis on which she received admiration. In Ethiopia family is like a blanket and then you come to the States and you're forced to confront your identity for the first time and you become unsure of yourself." Except when she was with Trang, Sinedu was usually seen eating alone; on weekend nights she could be found studying in the Dunster House library.

While he never thought of Sinedu as a happy person, he says, it had never occurred to him she was particularly *un*happy. She was "calculated, confident, composed at all times. She seemed the most rational and least emotional person I knew. Perhaps she knew that I admired those qualities, and that's why she didn't confide her emotional turmoil in me. She gave the impression of being able to handle everything."

He was astonished when, after her death, he discovered that she had been seeing a psychologist at the University Health Services since freshman year, because he thought he had known her daily schedule by heart. He had never heard of any psychologists in Ethiopia, nor had he heard of depression before he came to America, or thought much about self-fulfillment. "Happiness is not an Ethiopian value," he says. "The essence of happiness has to do with freedom of choice and pursuing your own desires. Ethiopians are supposed to be responsible; that is the highest value. Sinedu took this sense of responsibility to a higher degree. She led her life with as little variation as possible."

He had admired the way in which "Sinedu maintained her autonomy and didn't become overly friendly to make other friends. I always felt she made her own decisions and, when you make American friends, you cannot stay wholly Ethiopian. You compromise your identity." But, in retrospect, he believes that Sinedu "went to great lengths to conceal her loneliness." He thinks "it could have been fear that if she did open up her emotional side she'd be opening up a void she'd have no way of filling." He was startled to hear that, when a student from ICS who had been accepted to Harvard called to talk to Sinedu, she had described the social life at college as difficult. And Sinedu's high school friend Lillian, who had gone to school in California, told him that Sinedu had called and begged her to try to transfer to Harvard—another fact Sinedu had concealed from him.

The final semester of her life, he had found out, she became involved in an evangelical Bible study group, which he feels could only be the product of desperation, as she was the only person he had ever known in Ethiopia who had said she did not believe in the Church. She said she didn't believe in a God who was punitive—that seemed too human to her.

He remembers the first time Sinedu introduced him to Trang. "I could see from the way Sinedu paid attention to her that Trang was someone she could feel secure with. She was a foreigner, very nice and reserved like her. All of her life, Sinedu had been unique. When you're an exemplary student in Ethiopia, all achievements and awards are made public. You are never like other students." He thinks that Sinedu had "a yearning to finally find someone just like her—an exclusive friend, someone on whom your existence depends, who becomes the person you rely on the most—your primary attachment."

I ask him what his friendship with Sinedu consisted of if she never confided in him. But the question puzzles him—they respected one another, he says. I tell him that I had always thought one of the definitions of friendship is a person in whom you can confide. The sharing of problems is the currency of American friendships, the ritual gift-giving of our culture. The look on Neb's face shows how distastefully alien the idea is to him.

"All Ethiopians have hardship in common," he says. "We don't think of it as something to talk about."

I ask what he knows of Sinedu's childhood—whether she could have suffered some kind of trauma or abuse. There is no concept of child abuse in Ethiopia; corporal punishment is the norm, but he didn't think Sinedu got punished much at home because she was such a good student. She described her mother as stern, driving her to excellence. He thinks the time of her father's imprisonment was difficult for her, but they never spoke much about it.

I ask if he has a copy of *Wax and Gold*, a classic study of Amharic culture by a Western anthropologist, Donald N. Levine, that people keep mentioning to me. Its thesis is that the central metaphor for Amharic culture is a type of ancient poetry, often taught in monasteries, called *sem imma wok* (wax and gold). The image is taken from the technique used to fashion gold figures, in which a wax model is made and then covered in wet clay. When the clay is fired the wax runs out a small hole. Molten gold is then poured through the hole into the cast, and when it sets, the mold is broken to reveal the figure.

In the poetry, *sem imma wok,* the outer apparent meaning of the words conceals an inner true and often opposite meaning. Ethiopians are said to use the technique in their daily speech, as well. For example, when Ethiopians want to insult one another, they sometimes conceal their meaning in the form of an overt compliment. Sinedu's cryptic note to *The Crimson* could be thought of, a teacher at ICS told me, as a kind of *sem imma wok.* Although *sem imma wok* dates back thousands of years, the ideology of secrecy was clearly reinforced by the terror of the Derg. Neb tells me there is a copy of the book in his father's library, but he does not want anyone to know that he has it because the book is banned—or was banned under the Derg, and he does not know whether the ban has been lifted.

One of the odd things about Ethiopian society is the general sense of anxiety about what is legal, which no one seems to know exactly how to find out. One day, when Neb and I are driving in his car, we are stopped by a policeman. Neb offers the man some money, but he refuses it and takes down the license plate number. Neb is confused and alarmed—what does the policeman want? Traffic citations in Ethiopia are all solicitations for bribes. The refusal of a bribe implies a larger, more ominous purpose.

The policeman stares at me suspiciously, trying to figure out who I am, sitting beside Neb in the car. I'm conscious suddenly of our proximity; the bare arms of my summer dress. Neb shakes his head no, and speaks rapidly in Amharic. In the hotel at night Ethiopian men come up to me and say, "Airline hostess?" and ask me to go upstairs with them. They offer Ethiopian women money, of course, but Western women are thought not to need money, but to do it for pleasure instead. One of them grabbed my hand and pointed to the lack of a ring by way of proof.

I still have not made contact with Sinedu's family. I had originally planned to ask Neb to help me, but Terefe Kerse (who had taught Neb as well as Sinedu) warned me against it, explaining that Neb was Eritrean and therefore Sinedu's family—who are Amhara—wouldn't trust him. Terefe's American wife, Maura McMillin, had been embarrassed and scolded him, pointing out that only Neb's *father* was Eritrean—and not even Eritrean, but Tigrayan, the ethnic group from the north who had overthrown the Derg and are currently in power. But Terefe reiterated, "If you want to talk to the family, listen to an Amhara."

I asked Terefe if he knew whether the family was currently in town—a question he found naive. "Where would they go?" he said. The roads to the north are all flooded in the rainy season, and people don't travel often anyway. Land mines are still threaded all through the countryside, the debris of war everywhere.

The first time I call I reach Sinedu's father, Tadesse Zelleke. I tell him I would like to talk with them and he tells me it is not possible and says good-bye. The next time I call, Sinedu's mother, Atsede, answers the phone.

"What's the use of talking about Sinedu?" she says sharply, in a thickened English. "I do not want to hear anything again. I do not want to speak or hear anything about Sinedu. It will not help us. It is better to forget. My husband is resting from the hospital; he has heart attack."

I suggest we could talk about Sinedu's life, rather than her death, but she says, "Talking about her will push me to be sad, will make me remember her again and to feel sad again. I don't want to hear anything; I don't want to discuss. I was sad very much, I am so shocked. My daughter did not do that and I don't want to read that. She was envied."

After I hang up, it occurs to me I will not be able to call them a third time.

E very place I go, I develop the habit of telling people—taxi drivers, maids, hotel guests—that I'm working on a story about Sinedu Tadesse, an Ethiopian girl who went to Harvard University and died. I'm astonished by how successful this method is, how often people have heard of her and have opinions as to what happened, and occasionally even contacts to suggest. Rumors function in Ethiopia in the same way the media do in ours. Neighborhoods are tightly knit; people know what happens to one another.

Early in the morning the day after a death, a horn is sounded, and a crier walks down each street, announcing the death. Funerals are held at four in the afternoon, the same day. People have to be buried immediately because there is no embalming process, and it is not a society in which events need to be scheduled far in advance. Everyone belongs to an *edar,* a funeral society, to which they pay dues, and which in return finances part of the expense of a huge Ethiopian funeral, providing rented chairs and tents and dishes and professional wailers to scream. Attendance at funerals is mandatory for members of the *edar* and taken note of. Yeshi Tekleab, a teacher at ICS, told me that it was hard for her to work for a foreign institution that didn't understand how often Ethiopians needed to go to funerals. Of course she gets tired of going sometimes, she says, but one has to belong to an *edar*—otherwise who would come to one's own funeral?

At Sinedu's funeral the grave had to be hastily redug because the American coffin the body had been shipped in was too large for an

Ethiopian grave. A small speech was read listing Sinedu's accomplishments: her scores in the eighth grade exam and scholarships to ICS and Harvard University. "While she was studying at Harvard University, an unfortunate accident happened," the speech concluded. Only the few mourners at the funeral connected with ICS knew the story from America. But the others had heard rumors.

The two most common theories in Ethiopia are that either Sinedu was a lesbian or that she was possessed by spirits. If she was a lesbian, people tell me in hushed tones, then she did the right thing to kill herself and the object of her shame. Ethiopian women stress that there are no lesbians in Ethiopia: it is a perversity of Western culture which, if Sinedu had fallen into, would have shattered her native self beyond repair. When Yeshi's daughter was going to school in the States, she told her to be careful, warning her that "they have things like lesbians there." In the village her husband grew up in, such people were stoned. Another woman tells me about an article in an Amharic paper about a homosexual who said that he had the spirit of a woman trapped in a man's body. "So you see," she explained, "homosexuality is a form of spirit possession."

Neb finds it hard to conceive of Sinedu as a lesbian because he doesn't think of Ethiopian women like Sinedu as being particularly sexual. (Indeed, female sexuality is so feared in Ethiopia that almost all women have their genitals ritually mutilated, ordinarily at an age young enough so that they have never experienced orgasm.) As far as Neb knew, Sinedu never had or expressed interest in having a sexual relationship of any kind. She had told him that she might not get married and if she did it would be to a much older man—a fantasy he took not as a sign of being a lesbian, but of her basic fear of intimacy. There must be gay Ethiopians, Neb concedes, but they get married like everyone else because "it is not Ethiopian to give weight to your personal desires."

U nlike lesbianism, for which one is responsible, possession by spirits is regarded as a kind of casualty of living in the States; in Ethiopia it is common and curable. Through someone I meet at the hotel, I arrange for a meeting with a distant cousin of Sinedu's, a middle-aged woman who arrives clad in a red Western-style dress and high-heeled gold sandals. She tells me she does not wish her name to be written down, and that she is estranged from Sinedu's family, as are most of their relatives because Sinedu's mother quarreled with everyone when her husband was imprisoned. She is certain, however, she says, that had Sinedu stayed in Ethiopia this never would have happened. As soon as Sinedu started feeling bad, her parents would have taken her to the holy waters. But in America, what kind of help could she get? "In America, you have psychologists," she says, "but they don't have any special powers, do they?"

People are cured of spirits every week in the Ethiopian Orthodox Church—which practices an indigenous form of Christianity dating back to Ethiopia's conversion in A.D. 341. Ethiopians often express pride that they live in the only indigenous Christian African country. The Ethiopian Orthodox Church draws upon both Christian and Judaic practices, and includes draconian dietary laws, in which fasting occupies a half the year, and many labyrinthine rituals, usually described as incomprehensible to the uninitiated. In both theology and Ethiopian popular culture, the devil plays a central role. An Amharic saying for a quarrel is "The devil came between us."

In one form of spirit possession, Sinedu's cousin explains to me, the victim's soul is gradually replaced by a spirit of a foreign, evil nature, which leads them to do things more and more unlike themselves until they are finally driven to suicide and delivered into the hands of the devil—symptoms that perfectly fit the case of Sinedu. Sinedu had been the envy of many, with her scholarship to Harvard; a hex could easily have been placed upon her. Her transformation from a good girl from a good family into a killer seems clearly the work of unnatural forces.

Neb tells me that he doesn't believe in witchcraft. A woman he knew began acting strange and she was taken to the holy waters and the priest said he saw a spirit, and then shortly afterward she killed herself. But she had been abused as a child, he says, "so there was a Western explanation too." Once someone killed a chicken and sprayed the blood on Neb's family's gate and his mother was very frightened and went and got holy water to wash it off. But Neb says he's never heard of Americans being hexed or possessed by spirits, and "why would it only work in Ethiopia?" he asks.

Neb has, however, internalized the fear of envy so pervasive in the culture. He is very concerned that I not portray his family as too wealthy or fortunate. The fear of envy dates far back in Ethiopian culture, but it was reinforced by a communist regime which leveled everyone to poverty and persecuted and killed those who were better off. Even Ethiopians who do not specifically believe in witchcraft have a general superstitiousness of *kinat*—being "too much in people's eyes," that will make bad things happen to you—the sentiment Sinedu's mother was expressing when she told me on the phone that Sinedu was envied. And Sinedu was the envy of many, with her scholarship to Harvard—precisely the kind of person who attracts a hex. Social mobility, ambition, or even plans for the future are regarded suspiciously in Ethiopia, for rising is believed to pave the way for a downfall.

As a doctor, Sinedu would have supported her family. Instead they are left with grief and shame, the questions about her death, and the devastating expense of an Ethiopian funeral—the most costly event in a family's history, exceeding even the cost of a wedding. Several thousand people attended Sinedu's funeral, after which, as is customary, people drank coffee and ate *nufro*, wheat with chickpeas. Then large numbers of friends and relatives stayed with her family, sleeping in a tent in the courtyard; a second ceremony is planned for the fortieth day, when the gravestone is erected, and a third for the eightieth day.

The service was conducted by a priest, although suicides are not supposed to be given Christian burial because there is thought to be no point in praying for salvation for their souls: when the devil enticed the soul to suicide, he obtained it forever. In a course Neb took on revolutions, he learned that in Cuba it was a crime to try to commit suicide: if you were caught in the act, you would be sent to jail because your life doesn't belong to you, it belongs to the state. It's like that in Ethiopia, he says; your life doesn't belong to you, it belongs to your family and to the Church.

While suicide is very rare in Ethiopia, suicide rates are high among Ethiopians who emigrate to other countries, such as the United States and Israel. Ethiopian lives are like threads woven in a tapestry of suffering, Sinedu's cousin tells me. People always want to leave, but when you pluck the thread of their selfhood, it loses all meaning. She makes a pulling gesture with her fingers and opens her hands to show me there is nothing there.

It is time to talk to Sinedu's family. There's a rule of reporting that you can't give people an opportunity to say no to you too many times: if they hang up on you at first, you can call a second time, but if you call a third time they'll start to hate you. It's a problem reporters solve by a loathsome practice called "house-ends"—or uninvited visits—something I could never imagine myself doing.

Neb assures me that afternoon visits are an ordinary part of Ethiopian culture and that if I go at the proper hour the family will invite me in to partake of the afternoon coffee ceremony. "Be sure to go at the right hour," he stresses. I recall how Sinedu's cousins in Boston asked Harvard not to notify the family of Sinedu's death because the news is supposed to be brought by a relative, in person, in the morning. It had seemed strange to me then that the custom could be an important enough reason to delay notification of a death. When Dean Epps finally telephoned Sinedu's father to offer the college's condolences, he was startled by Tadesse Zelleke's graciousness; the first thing he did was to thank him for everything Harvard had done for his daughter.

"They can't turn you away," Neb says. "That would be very impolite. You are a foreigner too—a guest in our country."

So, I think, I'll be taking advantage of the conventions of their culture: acting in accordance with the rules of my own country, where the press is allowed to hound subjects, in a place where people can't be equally rude in return.

Days elapse while I contemplate this, wandering the streets, visiting schools and orphanages and medical clinics, faint and dazed from ten days of eating bananas—a fruit that doesn't require washing. I'm convinced that if I eat anything else I'll fall ill and end up in a hospital where the needles are risky, the blood supply contaminated with HIV—a punishment, perhaps, for my role in Ethiopia. Is imposing myself upon the family immoral? It's too late to worry about that now, though, I know—like a cop not answering a call his first day on the job because he's wondering whether he should become a social worker instead. And perhaps framing the question in moral terms is just a way to procrastinate about the real issue, which is simply whether I can do it—whether I am actually going to be able to knock on their door.

Here I am, though, halfway around the world on someone else's dime; am I really going to call the magazine and explain that I can't get the interview—and I can't even actually try?

I have a palpable sense, though, that to do this will cost me something, after which I will be left irreversibly less, although it is hard to say what exactly I am losing. My sense of myself as an empathetic person—different from the reporters swarming over campus in the days following the murder—not really a reporter at all? Writers are always selling someone out, Joan Didion wrote; it had never occurred to me, reading that years ago, that the first person the reporter has to sell is, of course, oneself.

Neb reassures me that there is nothing to be afraid of; Ethiopians are very hospitable, he says. He draws me an intricate map, using the embassies as landmarks. As in most African cities, all but a few streets in Ethiopia are unnamed because the city grew haphazardly and during the Derg regime the few signs that had been there were taken down because no one wanted to be found. Mail is sent to the post office where people pick it up. Most of the landmarks are foreign buildings; directions refer to charities, hotels, or the embassies which are dotted through the cities. Once I was given directions that referred to a hotel that I discovered—after wandering around for several hours—had disappeared a decade before. The Ethiopian who finally showed me the way didn't think the directions were odd—everyone knows, he said, where things used to be.

———

Afew days before my flight home I make my way to Sinedu's house. The dirt road is long and winding, past the open-sided tin shacks, dotted through Addis Ababa, that sell canned milk, cigarettes, soap, radio batteries. There is a butcher shack too, where a huge cow carcass hangs bloody on a hook, swarming with flies. Raw meat is a delicacy in Ethiopia; I've been offered it several times. Ethiopians love meat; the universal dish—*wat*—is a sauce with as much meat in it as they can afford.

Like all middle-class homes, Sinedu's family's house is surrounded by a high spiked gate to keep out intruders. I stand in the light afternoon rain, staring at the gate of scalloped tin, clutching a small bouquet of thorny roses. I had spent a long time trying to decide whether bringing a gift was too transparently manipulative. But it had also seemed to me inappropriate to arrive empty-handed—as if I were trying to take from their grief without acknowledging it. I had finally arrived at a little psychic compromise: I decided that if I bought the flowers myself and didn't charge the dollar twenty to my expense account that would make the gesture better.

As everywhere in Addis, the neighborhood is full of people. Passersby stare at me. An old man touches my shoulder, saying: "Peace Corps?" A crowd of bony barefooted children gather around, pulling at my damp skirt. A boy holding a black bull by a string speaks to me in Amharic, and then holds out his hand, begging.

I stand motionless in the rain. I am doing what I came to Ethiopia to do, I tell myself. But Sinedu has been buried less than a month. Suppose I had died and the press were knocking on my parents' door? But the family's loss is so absolute, it almost seems like arrogance to imagine anything I could do would add or detract from their tragedy—or make any difference to them at all.

Feeling faint, I knock softly on the tin gate. It opens and a young woman stands looking at me, soft and puzzled as a deer. I stammer something and she tells me she is Sinedu's sister Eskedar, and invites me to follow her inside.

The house is a classic Ethiopian construction, a low cement building within a walled courtyard. The small stone-walled living room is furnished with a few pieces of fifties-era American-style furniture and a small shelf of English books. Eskedar tells me that her mother—a nurse at a hospital—is at work and her father is asleep in the other room, recovering. I sit primly on the sagging couch while she goes to the kitchen and emerges, curiously, with a banana.

I manage to make conversation for a few moments, but I am terrified that we will wake her father and he will stumble out of the bedroom in his dressing gown and ask what I am doing there. I ask Eskedar to tell her parents I stopped by and wondered whether there was a better time to come back—a formulation the casualness of which I'm amazed I could come up with. If they don't invite me back, I think with relief, that will be it—I can tell myself I genuinely tried.

But Sinedu's father does call that night—to thank me for the flowers, he says. "My doctor has told me not to talk to any more reporters, but if it is your wish to talk to us, madam," he says, "you may come to our house tomorrow"—my last day in Ethiopia.

In the small yellow living room Sinedu's mother, father, two sisters, and a brother are gathered. There had been confusion about the time of the meeting because Sinedu's father had used Ethiopian time, which calculates the hour differently from official time, used by the government and the clocks at the Hilton Hotel. There is also a special Ethiopian calendar, based on a Julian calendar, according to which it is a different date—seven years and eight months behind. I ask the driver to wait for me; for a few dollars, a driver will wait all night.

Three of Sinedu's four older siblings live at home—Zenay, Sinedu's oldest sister, a judge, who studied law at the University of Addis Ababa; Amha, a brother who is studying business, and Eskedar, who studies accounting. Sinedu's brother Seiffe—a student at Dartmouth—is still in the States. Her father wears a traditional white cotton Ethiopian robe. He looks unwell, his movements stiff. The women all wear the long black mourning garb that is required for a year after a death. Sinedu's mother—a large woman with a hard face—cries silently into a handkerchief. Zenay serves orange Fanta and cookies.

One of them asks what I'm doing in Ethiopia, and unable to say the truth—I came to see you, to search for the origins of your daughter's pathology—I murmur something about researching a few different stories. I start telling them about a hospital I visited—the fistula hospital, founded by an Australian physician couple, which operates on women who have endured such prolonged labor that they have torn holes in their bladders and then become incontinent outcasts in their villages. I spoke with a woman who was in labor for three days, and after the baby was born dead she began leaking urine. Her husband kicked her out of the house because she smelled and the people in the village said she was cursed. She lived in a barn, begging for three years, in order to get the bus fare to go to the hospital in Addis Ababa for the repair.

"I don't care what a hundred police detectives or a thousand psychologists tell me," Sinedu's father announces without preface in a heavy, resounding voice, "I know my daughter did not commit these crimes. My daughter has been framed and murdered."

I lose my breath. All the questions I had prepared rested on the assumption that Sinedu was guilty, and that therefore in some way we were engaged in a common task of trying to understand what went wrong—why she did what she did. But if they believed she didn't do it, that changed everything.

I try to think of some neutral questions, like why Sinedu wanted to be a doctor or what courses she was taking—questions I already know the answer to—but they all meet with polite puzzlement.

"Children have their wishes and it was Sinedu's wish to be a doctor," her father said. "We supported her in that wish."

"But why a dermatologist?" Because ICS is near a leper colony? They shrug. The answer to so many questions is, "She never said." Was she religious? "She had all the necessary instruction." Was she happy at Harvard? "She never complained." She never spoke of any problems with her roommate? She told them her roommate was "very friendly and cooperative."

"The stories we read we do not believe. It is the opposite of the nature of Sinedu. Who would know her if not her parents?" her father says with urgency. "Her mother and I? We have been with her all of her life. We eat from the same table," he says, stumbling, unable to explain the cord of connection they feel, from which it is incomprehensible she could have willingly severed herself.

"There has been a cover-up," Sinedu's father says in a heavy final voice, and instructs me to search out the truth. I suggest they could ask Harvard more questions about Sinedu, but he says bitterly, "They will not tell us anything." He tells me that he wrote Harvard a letter in which he said that the murder had been the result of a setup, a plot to destroy his daughter, but Harvard prefers to blame his daughter and look no further. Eskedar also wrote a letter to which she received a brief response from L. Fred Jewett, '57, then dean of Harvard College, in which he said that he was writing on behalf of

President Rudenstine to say that Harvard could not comment on any aspect of the investigation and they should direct their questions to the district attorney's office.

"I know the States," he says. "Things are very closed there. Things cannot be found out."

I hesitate, and then say faintly, "But you read the news stories?"

"No."

I have the file in my hotel room—stories that reveal the facts for which there is no other scenario than that Sinedu was the perpetrator: the barricaded door, the locked windows, the witness.

I nod, uneasily. Should I be collaborating in their denial or ought I to be, in some way, acting as an advocate of reality? What if I convince them and their faith in Sinedu collapses and destroys them? What if her father has another heart attack? Perhaps their reluctance to let me into their house was a desire to keep this knowledge outside—knowledge that may be unbearable. Abruptly I rise to go.

Zenay walks me to the gate, in the thick night air, where the driver waits for me.

"I know it is God's will that my little sister died on that day," she says, resting her hand on the gate, the black silk of her robe glinting in the moonlight. "My parents are just waiting for the truth to be revealed. Perhaps through you the truth will come to light."

"Perhaps," I say. She closes the gate behind me. The vast Ethiopian night enfolds me in its blinding embrace, and I stumble forward toward the shallow light of the waiting car.

THREE

TRANG

*B*oston magazine's February 1992 issue was a special thirtieth-anniversary issue with a cover story entitled "25 Who Can Save Boston." The magazine had culled a list of twenty-five "local heroes and heroines"—people who "hold Boston's future—your future and ours—in their hands." The people profiled were predictable luminaries at the pinnacle of their careers, men and women chosen on the basis of accomplishments and contributions: the mayor, the governor, the cardinal, the presidents of MIT and Boston University, a senator, the CEOs of major corporations. The final entry, however, the twenty-fifth, is: "Postscript: Trang Ho, 18, Harvard Freshman," and it is she who has been chosen as the representative of the next generation—of promise not yet fulfilled.

Regarding her future, she says she is thinking about becoming either a doctor or a scientist. Either way, though, she intends to remain in Boston.

"You've got to have some people who stay behind," she says. "You need people who are committed and want to make a change, and not give up and go somewhere else. One thing in my life I don't like to do is give up."

In retrospect, this little piece of magazine inspiration seems in some way to have captured the essence of Trang's voice—her willfully optimistic outlook. It reminds me of a discussion about immigration and the boat people I once heard on television; the American dream has to be continually imported, a woman was saying. "We *need* immigrants—they bring us hope." I was struck by the curiousness of this sentiment: why do we need to import hope? And why would they be more likely to have it, these immigrants fleeing poverty and war? I look at Trang's life—crossing the ocean to arrive without money or language in a strange land, her family twice separated—and I wonder what gave her that extraordinary quality: a faith that seems to shine all the more clearly and mysteriously in the light of her fate.

T rang's father, Phuoc Xuan Ho, was raised by relatives in a poor family in central Vietnam. His father had been a road builder who died young, and his mother had been taken away by the communists and sent to a "reeducation camp." Trang's mother, Quy Huynh, grew up in a wealthy educated family, the beautiful daughter of a governor of a district, who later lost his position and money when the communists came to power. Phuoc and Quy were high school sweethearts; they married in 1972 in the town of Trung Hieu. Phuoc went to the University of Saigon to study architecture and Quy became a schoolteacher.

In 1970, Phuoc joined the South Vietnamese Navy, fighting the communists who had imprisoned his mother. Their first child, Thao, was born in 1973. Trang was born the following year, in the year of the Tiger, which prophesied, Trang's mother recalls, that girls born that year would be extraordinary. Five months later Saigon fell to the North Vietnamese and Phuoc and Quy were placed in "reeducation" camps—forced labor camps in which prisoners were starved and tortured. However, Phuoc was quickly released because he was disabled—he had been shot in the stomach and arm during the war. Quy was kept for six months, but then released because she was a teacher—a skill the new regime needed. A few years later a third daughter, Tram, was born.

Phuoc was given permission to live in a city where it was impossible to find work, so he moved the family illegally to Ho Chi Minh City, where he worked as a businessman. Quy was sent to teach in another part of Vietnam, leaving the little girls to be cared for by their grandparents. "Due to circumstances, we had no childhood," Thao says. Their apartment was near the hospital; day and night they heard the screech of ambulances. From as early as Thao can remember, Quy and Phuoc's marriage was filled with discord. "My dad is typical Asian guy," Thao says. "He control the power, expect the woman to do what he wants. My mom, she is independent."

As a child, Thao says, she was her father's favorite; Tram, the baby, was her mother's favorite and Trang was "pretty much on her own." Thao remembers Trang as "very strong—she stick up for what she does, what she believes is right, she not apologize." As a result, Trang was frequently punished both by their father and at school. In the rigid educational system teachers were "like gods," and each pupil was given a numerical ranking. In her class of fifty, crammed in the small classroom, Thao always ranked first or second, but Trang was ranked in the twenties.

Her mother recalls Trang as a generous, peacemaking child. When other children fought at school, she would always tell her mother how upset she was when she came home. When her mother would give money to beggars, Trang would always tell her that it wasn't enough. She liked animals; the family raised birds and fish and one day, when her parents were at work, Trang let them all go. Thao remembers how their mother bought Trang a skirt that Thao liked and she complained to her mother and Trang gave her the skirt. Trang was fascinated by the ocean; her mother remembers Trang telling her once how the ocean was like the world to her—vast and mysterious, filled with things she wanted to discover.

Throughout the girls' childhood their parents spoke of escape to America. Because Quy worked for the government as a teacher, she and Phuoc were able to open a coffee shop without harassment from the government, and they began to rebuild the savings they had lost in the war—money they would need to escape.

When Trang was two, they attempted an escape in a small fishing boat with Quy's parents. At one point, Trang fell overboard and was rescued by her grandfather. But the Viet Cong were all around and they had to turn back. Several other attempts also failed. Finally, in 1984, when Trang was nine, Phuoc resolved to try again, taking the two eldest girls. When they got established in America, they would sponsor Quy and Tram to join them. Quy didn't want to leave without her parents. It was also very dangerous to try to escape as a whole family because, if the family was caught, they would need some members to act as advocates and try to bribe officials to let them out of jail.

E arly in the morning of December 17, 1984, Phuoc and the girls took a bus to a village in central Vietnam, where they spent a few days with relatives. One night, while they were sleeping, their uncle cut Thao's and Trang's hair to make them look like boys, to protect them against rape by pirates during the voyage. Then came the evening of departure. They took a bus to a deserted beach where they hid among rocks. At eleven o'clock at night, after they waited five hours, a small boat pulled up to the shore. They all crept on to the unsturdy vessel; no one in the family could swim. The girls were certain they would never see their mother again. The boat took them out to sea where a larger ship was waiting, crammed with two hundred and sixty-five others, heading toward Indonesia.

The seas were calm on the evening of departure, but they were terrified they would be discovered. At one point they glimpsed a government boat following them and changed direction. Finally they crossed the line into international waters and knew they were free. The ship was so crowded that the family had to stand for the entire seven days; the father stood in front of the little girls to protect them from the waves. During the day Phuoc went around to the other passengers and collected water for them to drink.

Two days into the voyage, the weather turned rough. People huddled through the storm, and then the boat hit a barrier reef, with a terrible sound of collision. The entire boat began to pray, believing they were about to die. And then, suddenly, the storm ended and everything went back to normal. It was Christmas Eve; they knew it was a miracle.

After six nights and seven days they reached a refugee camp on Galang Island, Indonesia. The atmosphere at the camp was violent and dangerous; Phuoc kept close to his daughters at all times. Thao recalls the camp as hot and dirty; the girls were frequently sick. During the day they all studied English. The girls were the top students in the class, which made Phuoc very happy. Each day he would give his daughters additional vocabulary to memorize from a textbook: at first ten or twenty words a day, and then a hundred. They talked constantly about when they would get out of the camp and their lives would begin.

Finally, in November 1985—after eleven months—their visas came through and they flew to San Diego. Thao remembers her amazement at seeing the city for the first time: the highway, the way everything went so quickly. They stayed in the room of a Vietnamese family, which their sponsor—a friend of a friend—found for them. Trang baby-sat for the family's children: Trang was good with kids, Thao said—she herself would watch.

Supported by public assistance, Phuoc took English classes and the girls were enrolled in a public school. Their first semester at school was difficult. Thao felt timid, but Trang was more outgoing and adapted better. Trang took her homework very seriously and was determined to do it well, although she barely knew the language. Displaying the traits that would one day get her into Harvard, once when Trang was stuck on her homework, she called 911 for assistance. A minute later the phone rang, and Phuoc heard an officer on the line asking for the little girl who needed help with her homework.

After about a year, Phuoc decided to move the family to Boston, where he had heard it was easier to get work. He had also heard of all the famous universities in Boston he dreamed his daughters might one day attend. They moved into a three-decker, a few blocks from the Ashmont station in Dorchester, a working-class community, with a large Vietnamese population.

Phuoc studied electrical engineering at Bunker Hill Community College and at Wentworth Institute of Technology. Thao and Trang were as diligent in their schoolwork as he could hope; once they were watching a television program, and he recalls how, without prompting, they turned the show off halfway through when they realized it was eight o'clock, the time appointed for homework. Trang and Thao were both admitted to the public John D. O'Bryant School of Mathematics and Science (then called Boston Technical High School)—an exam school in Roxbury oriented toward the sciences. Trang rose to the top of her class and received academic awards all four years. "Trang really began to blossom intellectually when we came to the States," Thao said. "She became very straightforward and honest, confident and single-minded."

Although Thao had felt she had been her father's favorite in Vietnam, in America she felt he and Trang had developed a closer bond. "My dad believes girls should be studious and obedient and not go out or have a social life," Thao says. "Trang she really listen to

him. I don't believe that at all—you have to have a social life." Thao
had boyfriends in high school and in college—a source of tension in
the family. Trang did not. Trang was always telling her sister, "Remember, you don't just have a boyfriend; you have a future." In
Vietnamese culture, if a bride is found not to be a virgin, the marriage
can be dissolved; Trang believed sex outside marriage was wrong.

When Phuoc graduated from Bunker Hill, Trang wrote him a
congratulatory card in English:

> Hello Pop!
>   Yes, you did it! I am so happy for you. I'm always
> honored to be a daughter of an intellectual man. I love you!!!
>   Trang

Phuoc says he tried to be "both a mother and a father" to his
daughters. "He was a good father," Thao says. "He cooked and took
care of us. He would learn to cook different dishes to try to make us
happy. He'd come check on us when we were sleeping and see if we
were too hot or too cold." On weekends, he took them on nature
walks. The girls missed their mother very much. After they left
Vietnam, their mother had been harassed by the government for the
crime of her husband's escape. The family worked actively to get
their mother brought over, with Trang writing letters to Senator
Kennedy. However, because they were on public assistance, they
couldn't sponsor her.

Every four or five years a student gets into Harvard from the
John D. O'Bryant School of Mathematics and Science, a
school with an overwhelmingly minority population, located
in Roxbury, a low-income area of Boston. Trang Ho was the last such

student, and her teachers—with whom she had kept in touch, visiting and sending cards—were devastated by the murder. "It was almost surreal to us. Why would it happen to someone we held so dear?" Clifford Wong, one of her guidance counselors, asks. A dozen teachers attended her wake, and when Mr. Wong passed the hat for the Trang Ho Family Fund, he raised more than a thousand dollars.

"She was a very thoughtful young woman to go along with all that ability. I've never seen an individual so cherished by her teachers. She created a certain expectation for students I haven't seen again. There have been other students who excelled academically, but they didn't have that total package. Her determination to succeed; her friendliness as a person—she was a totally friendly individual, outgoing enough to reach out to so many students and teachers. She was so organized and so pleasant—sometimes she'd pay me homage and ask me for guidance—I think she knew the answers before I gave them, but asked to make me feel good, which was just like her. Yeah, we miss her," he said, his voice breaking. "She was the daughter everyone wishes to have."

Her English teacher, Crystal Coy-Gonfa, says that "some of the kids you see here, you're not that surprised when they end up on the six o'clock news for something negative. But not Trang Ho," she says, shaking her head, bewildered. She recalls her as "always moving—this little tiny girl coming down the hallway, her backpack filled with books, moving quickly—she always had so many places to get to. I guess she's not going to get to any of them now."

Along with her courses, Trang was involved in a whirlwind of activities. She organized a poetry club and also a Ping-Pong and badminton club, the "Pington Club," for which she served as treasurer. She took courses at Simmons College and volunteered at the Spaulding Rehabilitation Hospital. She participated in a program at Massachusetts General Hospital for students interested in medicine, and received a summer stipend to work in a research lab under the guidance of a biochemist.

None of the teachers ever met Phuoc. Although there were a number of scheduled parent/teacher conferences each year, Phuoc never went to any of them. This is characteristic of Asian families, John Guaragna, Trang's math teacher, tells me, "because the children often speak better English than their parents do. That's the incredible combination you see in so many Asian families," he says. "The students are self-motivated because their parents can't take over their studies, but the parents are totally behind them emotionally, pushing them, instilling educational values."

"She was a very aggressive learner," says one of Trang's English teachers, Paul Lyons. "She had this almost tactile style of learning. She wouldn't be content—she'd pursue things. She'd attack the subject for the depth of the material. She'd learn the vocabulary and then you'd actually see the words start to show up in her writing and hear her using them conversationally. When she read a book she liked, she'd get others by the same author. She'd make her Vietnamese friends talk English—she recognized that as a trap. She was very positive and upbeat, but also humble and unassuming."

Philip Hughes, Trang's science teacher, says, "When she'd get a question wrong, she'd take it as a challenge to find out more about that topic. She'd come to you and want to know why—in a mild, not a confrontational way. A lot of kids say they want to be a doctor, but with Trang, I never doubted it for a moment."

"She was always asking why, why, why?" Denise Traniello, a science teacher who taught a course in medical technology, says. "She could talk Pontius Pilate out of doing it: 'Now why do you want to crucify him, on this cross, as opposed to this other form of punishment, and is that really right?' She'd ask what causes this disease, and I'd say medicine is not an exact science. I always thought she'd be a good pathologist because only pathology is an exact science, but she wanted to be a pediatrician."

Whereas Sinedu's academic success seems to have stunted her emotional development, for Trang the two nurtured one another. Rather than isolating her, her success allowed her to reach out to others. Throughout high school she was always tutoring her classmates. When she went to see Mr. Wong, she would end up helping other students with their college applications while she waited her turn. Denise Traniello remembers being irritated because the other students were copying Trang's work, using her not to get help but to crib from. "But Trang was too innocent," she says, "she'd never see it. Before she saw evil, she always saw good."

During Trang's senior year she applied to a half dozen colleges. Thao—who had been the valedictorian of her own class—had applied and been rejected by Harvard, but she felt that Tufts, where she had gone, was better suited to her anyway. Trang, however, had her heart set on Harvard.

Phuoc remembers looking at Trang's Harvard application and feeling extremely impressed. Written in the slightly stiff language of an immigrant taught in a high school English class, Trang's application essay is nevertheless a stirring document. Although she begins by stating that she is a refugee, her subject is not her own experience, but rather the plight of other refugees and the new laws restricting the immigration of the boat people.

"Without the help of advocates, my family would still be in a camp, striving against all odds for survival and not having the opportunity to succeed as I have now," she wrote. "I am grateful for their help. Although I no longer live in Vietnam, I still care for my countrymen. I will never forget the fact that I was a refugee, nor will

I ever forget that I am one of the leaders of the future who will make significant differences."

The admissions office at Harvard (whose stated goal is to "identify future world leaders") immediately recognized the qualities they were looking for in Trang. "We thought: here is this person with all this potential to do a lot for herself and for others," recalls a former admissions officer. "She was this beacon from Boston—a future leader of the Boston Vietnamese community. People liked her and were drawn to her friendliness."

In response to the Harvard application question about one's favorite books, Trang mentioned a few classics and then focused on how "at Harvard and Radcliffe I'd like to share the knowledge I've acquired and the writing skills I have obtained with the students in the Refugee Youth Enrichment Program (RYSE). I know how difficult it is for new refugees to learn a new language, so I'd like help them overcome that difficulty." For her, the primary purpose of reading and writing seems to have been to help others do those things.

She was accepted by every college she applied to, with special recruiting phone calls from Harvard and Brown, both of which offered her full scholarships. According the the *New York Times*, the admissions office gave Trang one of the two highest overall rankings in her class of thirteen hundred students. The Harvard admissions office scores people in four separate areas: academics, extracurricular, athletics, and personal qualities, and then rates each applicant with an overall score. The former admissions officer recalls that Trang scored the highest in the category of personal qualities. "On the academic side she could have been better prepared," he says, "but her personal characteristics told you where she was going."

At graduation, Trang received "first and second place in the Dupont Regional Science Essay Contest; first in the Black History

Month Essay Contest; the Citizenship Award; the Harvard Alumni Book Award; and high honors all four years. She opened her high school valedictorian speech with the quote: "I am the master of my fate; I am the captain of my soul."

Sitting in the front row, listening to Trang were her mother and youngest sister. Her English teacher, Crystal Coy-Gonfa, recalls how Trang used to "write essays about how much she wanted and needed her mother in her life—she thought all her problems would be solved by having her mother here. I always saw her comforting others—I wondered who was comforting her." Tears came to Crystal Coy-Gonfa's eyes when she saw the family had been reunited; she thought Trang's mother had finally arrived just in time to watch Trang graduate, the star of her class.

What none of her teachers knew was that Trang's mother had actually arrived eight months before—the previous October—and that the long-awaited reunion had been a devastating event, resulting in a permanent separation of the family.

T he Ho family file in the Middlesex family and probate court contains a sad narrative. The card catalogue of 1992 probate cases, lists half a dozen cards for Ho, and then "Ho, Phuoc vs. Quy Huynh," with a docket number, under which their case is filed. I had been dimly aware that divorce proceedings are generally publicly available, but it is startling to see how easily they can be obtained. There in the folder is a wrinkled yellow paper of the Ho marriage certificate, in Vietnamese, next to a certified translation, and the few dozen papers—letters from doctors, and lawyers and financial statements—which record their family history.

In 1989 Quy had gathered the money to buy her way out of

Vietnam. She had made several previous attempts at escape, including trying to reach Thailand by walking to Cambodia. She was captured near the border, but because it was New Year's Day, the soldiers let her go. By the time Quy and Tram arrived in a labor camp in Malaysia, U.S. immigration policy had become much more restrictive (the very policy which was the subject of Trang's Harvard application essay, although she does not explain that one of the refugees whose plight she described was her mother). It was more than three years before they obtained permission to emigrate

Almost immediately, however, Quy and Phuoc's reunion turned bitter. Within days, they began fighting, with allegations of infidelity on Phuoc's part. Trang became ill with anxiety and took to bed. A week later, according to charges Quy filed, Phuoc threatened her with a knife. She took Tram, fled to a shelter in Medford, and filed for a restraining order. In much of Vietnam, wife beating is customary, but Quy knew that it was a crime in the new country. Less than a month after her arrival, a court judgment was handed down: Quy was given custody of Trang and Tram, the two minors, and Phuoc was ordered not to come within two hundred yards of the house for one year.

Quy moved the girls to Medford and Phuoc stayed behind in their apartment in Dorchester. Trang told no one at school about the troubles at home—or even that her mother had arrived in the country. With her father gone and Thao at Tufts, the burden of caring for her mother and sister, who spoke no English in the new country, fell to Trang. "Breaking up and not being a family really bothers Trang," Thao recalls. "Trang get really sick the first few months. She would break down, and on top of that she was applying to colleges. I was amazed at the end of the year how she pulled it all off and went to Harvard."

Both girls struggled to reconnect with the mother and sister they hadn't seen since they were children. "My mom—before I left I was very close to her," Thao says, "but when she came things had changed. We hadn't seen Tram for ten years, we miss her so much, we had all that longing to see her again, but when she came we realized we didn't know her."

Feeling shamed in the community, Phuoc moved to San Diego that summer, before the dreamed-of day his daughter moved into Harvard Yard. For Trang, the price of her mother's return was the loss of the parent on whom she had relied all these years.

After she went to Harvard, Trang continued to go home each weekend to teach her little sister Tram English, to do paperwork for her mother, and to help with the housework. The family survived on public assistance, along with money Trang earned from her jobs at school. The papers her mother filed for divorce stated: "Husband has been physically abusive towards wife throughout the marriage. During the time that the parties both resided in Vietnam, Husband hit Wife on numerous occasions and slammed her head into walls. Husband has also threatened to disfigure Wife and to physically harm her family members."

Phuoc replied to the judge at the Middlesex court:

"Starting from the date of reunion, my wife began her cold treatment towards me. On the night of November 3, 1991, when I could no longer stand the way she treated me, I suddenly got mad momentarily and called the police. When the police came, I realized I was in a hot temper. However, it would not be fair to say that I am 'guilty of cruel and abusive treatment,' as stated on the Complaint for Divorce. The following day, my wife suddenly went to court while I went to school. Since then, our family problem evolved. I think that there has been something wrong in either my mind or my wife's. . . .

"The hurt of a man without his family is like that in the story of 'The Man Without A Country.' Family is very important to human beings. . . .

"I always love my family: My children and my wife, Quy Thi Huynh. But however she wants to solve this family problem such as reuniting or even divorcing is fine with me under the permission of the court."

The document was accompanied by a doctor's certificate diagnosing Phuoc with depression. The divorce was granted in January 1994 on the grounds of "cruel and abusive treatment," with no order of support, as Phuoc was then on welfare. Quy was granted sole custody of the remaining minor child, Tram; Phuoc was given no visitation rights.

After the divorce, Thao says, she found it was too difficult to keep in touch with her father: "Trang the only one who keep in touch with him. She sent him cards and sign all our names, but I never knew about any of them."

What is striking about Trang's notes to her father is the way in which they attempt to negotiate his losses for him, reassuring him of his daughters' love for him, through the separation.

After one fight, she wrote to her father in Vietnamese, on a card decorated with hearts and a bear:

May 7, 1994

I've missed you very much. I'm sorry we won't be able to see you again. However we couldn't get along on the phone,

you are always my good father and you are always in my
heart.

But the card her father rereads most often now is:

Dear Ba Kinh-nho [Father]

It Takes A Lifetime

It takes a lifetime to learn
how to live,
How to share and how to give,
How to face tragedy that
comes your way,
How to find courage to
face each new day,
How to smile when your heart
is sore,
How to laugh when you want
to cry,
How to be brave when you
say goodbye,
How to still love when your
loss is so great. . . .

We hope that this poem by Ruth Moyer Gilmour would
cheer you up. We are always thinking of you. . . . Love,
Thao, Tram, Trang.

———

Trang's friend Khoi Luu says that he particularly admired the way "Trang didn't share her pain with anyone. She was able to laugh a lot. Those are the two things I remember about her the most—her smile and her strength. I think they're related, I think people who have a lot of pain appreciate laughter."

Khoi knows about pain; his father had fought on the side of the Americans and after the war was over, when Khoi was three, he was sent to a reeducation camp. Khoi and his mother waited four years for his father to be released until they got a letter from him telling them to go visit his brother. His brother lived in Kansas; they knew he meant not to wait for him any longer. They left for America and shortly afterward received word of his death. Like Trang, Khoi feels an obligation to succeed to redeem the hardship of his mother's life in America. He wants to be a writer, but he is going to law school so that he can support his mother, who works as a seamstress.

Trang's friend Huong Mai remembers how sometimes she would catch Trang looking down and she would ask her what she was thinking of. " 'I'm just a little sad right now,' Trang would say, but she would never tell anyone what she was sad about. She seemed happy, but she wasn't happy. She have many burdens, she care about her family all the time. I would tell her, 'You have to concentrate on yourself, you can't make everything right for them,' but her family is all she think about."

One person in whom Trang confided was Jim Igoe, an engineer at Polaroid whom she had met on a field trip her junior year in high school. Their relationship is a good example of Trang's ability to seek out the nurturing she needed from teachers and mentors. "It was a very unique relationship," Jim Igoe says, "and I was the luckiest man in the world to have it. Right from the beginning, we just seemed to connect in this special way."

After the school tour of the Polaroid lab, Trang had come up to him and begun asking him "all these incredible questions." He had showed the students a chemical reactor, which controlled the temperature of all the chemicals, and she wanted to know how it worked and why it was accurate. When he explained that it was being calibrated, she wanted to know how calibration worked. "I'm thinking: this is a junior in high school," he says. "Then she wanted to have her picture taken with me, and asked if she could call me to talk more about engineering and I gave her my card. By the time Polaroid served pizza to the kids, I had a buddy for life."

After that, they began to do things together in Dorchester, where they both lived—going to the Dorchester Flower Show and other cultural events and to museums. He had been recently separated from his wife, and they'd both talk about their family troubles. He would ask her for advice about his daughter and what she was going through, sometimes in the form of hypothetical questions like, "What if you were my daughter and I had to work all the time to send you to a good school so you didn't get to see me—how would you feel about that?" And Trang would reply, "I'd understand." She'd also tell him, "Don't treat your daughter as naive—she understands more than you think."

Whenever they went places, she would never let him pay for her museum tickets or meals. He knew that her family had financial problems, but they never talked about it. "She was very proud and would always deny it," he said. Sometimes he'd go over to their home and the heat would be turned off. Quy would tell him that there was something wrong with the furnace, and he'd check it and there would never be anything wrong with it.

Trang would often ask him about aspects of Western culture. She loved slang, he says, and she would ask what certain phrases meant and then practice them with him. After she went to college, she began to ask him about boys. She had crushes on Khoi Luu and Hans Stohrer, and she'd ask for his advice, but he knew she had traditional values and didn't really want a romantic involvement.

He discouraged her from pursuing engineering: "Her mind was much too unique for that. I always felt she was extremely brilliant and imaginative," he says. Part of her gift, he felt, was her ability to imagine her future and to believe that she had a destiny: that—as she said in her valedictory speech—she was the master of her fate, the captain of her soul.

"You could discuss anything with her—conversation was the stars for her. I loved to watch her mind at work. She'd always look up at me with her glasses crooked and I'd straighten them out for her. It was like she was always so absorbed in the world, she couldn't be bothered to do it. When we went to the Museum of Fine Arts, she'd stare at the paintings and then close her eyes and visualize being in the world of the painting."

He recalls a painting Trang particularly loved of a woman and her young daughter in a rowboat by Edmund Tarbell, a turn-of-the-century American Impressionist. In the painting, the mother is steadying a little girl in a starchy white dress who is standing straight up, staring directly ahead, her eyes a piercing blue. The water all about them is alight with sun, but the boat is at an odd angle to the canvas, lurching forward and downward, into the shadow of a cluster of overhanging branches—nearing a shore, perhaps, an unknown harbor. The prow is cut off by the bottom of the canvas—as if the tip

MELANIE THERNSTROM

of the boat is too near for sight and the journey into a darkened future collides, invisibly, into us.

T he last time Jim Igoe spoke to Trang was a few days before she died. When the phone rang at one or two in the morning, he knew it was Trang because no one else ever called that late. She told him she had taken one exam and was worried about the others—that she wouldn't perform her best. He told her to relax and go for the B's instead of the A's, but she felt an obligation to live up to her scholarship and not let Harvard down. Her sisters were fighting at home, she told him, and she was worried about the troubles there. As she talked, she began to cry. But even during this most vulnerable moment, he recalls, as she poured out her troubles to him, she never once mentioned her roommate.

"Of all the troubles she knew she had," he says, "Sinedu was never one of them."

FOUR

HARVARD

In the president's traditional welcoming speech to Harvard freshmen, he tells the class that all new students secretly believe that they are the admission committee's one mistake. However, he announces, in a voice of gravitas: *"There are no admissions mistakes. Each and every one deserves to be here."*

The endowing of specialness—the sense of Harvard admission as an important and irrevocable stamp of approval—is impressed upon students at every turn. "John F. Kennedy Slept Here. So Did Ralph Waldo Emerson and FDR. And Very Soon You," read the headline in *The Crimson* welcoming Sinedu and Trang's class to campus in 1992. "There you will find yourself," an old man instructs Thomas Wolfe's protagonist in *Look Homeward, Angel,* for, Wolfe writes, Harvard was not merely "the name of a university. It was rich magic, wealth, elegance, joy, proud loneliness, rich books and golden browsing; it was an enchanted name like Cairo and Damascus."

It was the fifth year in a row that Harvard had been named by *U.S. News & World Report* the nation's number one school and the fifth consecutive year it had a record number of applicants. Only fourteen percent of its applicants were accepted. More tellingly, it has a yield rate of almost eighty percent (the term colleges use to refer to the percentage of students who accept their offers of admission)— significantly higher than any of its competitors. In short, few students accepted at Harvard choose to go elsewhere; as the title of a cover story in *New York* magazine expressed the sentiment: "Give Me Harvard or Give Me Death." As a Harvard administrator explains, "There is a growing perception that the Harvard degree is a special advantage, as evidenced in the fact that the yield keeps going up. The yield is a measure of people's perception. What it translates into in real terms is the quality of the student body. Assembling a student body seems to be the one thing Harvard does to perfection."

She sees this as partly a function of economics. While the country is not in a depression, it is a time of widespread economic anxiety. "In a vocational era, people know a Harvard degree translates into money," she says. "A Harvard degree comes close to guaranteeing you have a good start. Nothing else has that ring of ultimate success. It is the only college in America with international value and recognition. In practically any field, you have a base of contacts with which to begin."

Historians often describe Harvard's historic preeminence as a function of its twofold appeal of venerability and accessibility—its association with both Puritans and Jews. On the one hand, the nation's first college continued to appeal to the elite, many of whose families had long relationships with the school. The postwar association with the Kennedys cemented the idea of Harvard as Camelot in the popular imagination. But Harvard also drew talent from minorities who found doors closed to them elsewhere. Harvard abandoned an important symbol of its original Christian identity in 1886 when it abolished compulsory attendance at chapel, three decades before Yale and half a century before Princeton did. Its informal quota on the number of Jewish undergraduates was much less restrictive than that of other Ivy League colleges. It was able to skim off the cream of the educated Jewish refugee families who fled the Nazis. By the late 1950s Jewish students were as much as forty percent of the student body— two to three times that of Yale and Princeton. The school's relative liberality was rewarded with generous donations from wealthy Jewish families like the Loebs and the Pforzheimers. Many Jewish graduates of the college went on to prominent careers in Hollywood and the media, and mythologized their school by making it the subject of movies and articles.

Harvard has retained a special appeal for minorities and international students. Foreign students make up seven percent of the Harvard student body today. Minorities constitute over a third, with

Asians representing by far the largest share (nineteen percent of Harvard students, although they constitute only three percent of the population at large.) As the Vietnamese owner of a dry cleaning establishment explained his disappointment at his son's acceptance to Yale: "Relatives in Vietnam not heard of Yale."

"Harvard has a special mythical dimension that other schools don't have to deal with," the administrator explains. "Students arrive at this legendary place and they are all thrown together under the bland assumption that the magic of multiculturalism will work its influence. And sometimes it does and sometimes it doesn't. Students who don't fit in can feel very isolated and lost."

The terrible news that awaited Sinedu when she arrived at Harvard was that, although she had left a great many things behind, she had brought her problems with her. The loneliness she had suffered in Ethiopia intensified, and the academic reinforcement she had relied upon disappeared. She did not feel close to her freshman roommate and she did not know how to make other friends. She found the climate inhospitable; her clothing was inadequate for the New England winter, and she had no money for new things. The dreamed-of land had turned out—as in a dream—to resemble the inner landscape in which she had dwelt all her life: impoverished, isolated, and entrapping.

Ethiopians who go to college in the States often find themselves suffering from an isolation they are culturally unprepared for. Dr. Tedla Wolde Giorgis, an Ethiopian psychologist, puts it thus: "There is no tradition of rugged individualism in Ethiopia. Ethiopians' self-identity lies in their community. In America, you believe, 'I think, therefore I am,' as Descartes says, but in Ethiopia we believe, 'We think, therefore we are.' In America, there is the great loss of the we."

Organization like the African Students Association don't solve the problem because Ethiopians don't identify with other Africans, with whom they don't share a language, common history, or culture any more than Americans do with Mexicans. Some Ethiopians actually take offense as being referred to as African, saying, "Not African, Ethiopian." They feel pushed toward the larger African-American community, which they feel their culture is radically different from, and there aren't enough Ethiopians at most colleges to form their own community.

For the first time in their lives, many Ethiopians find racial identity has been thrust upon them. One Ethiopian-American student tells me how she would never fill out forms inquiring about ethnic origins, until someone in the financial aid office explained to her that her scholarship was dependent on her classification as a minority. Most Ethiopians have never thought of themselves as black: in Ethiopia they are Amharic, Tigrayan, or Oromo.

Racism is something Ethiopians often experience for the first time in America. Ethiopians take strong national pride in belonging to the only African country never to be colonized by whites (although this is not, strictly speaking, true—there was a brief period of Italian rule from 1936 to 1941). Adey Fisseha, an Ethiopian-American member of the African Students Association whose family emigrated to America when she was a child, says, "The longer you're in the U.S., the more your sense of color consciousness tends to develop. For African-Americans, racism has been an active part of their growing up, but in Ethiopia it's not a factor."

An Ethiopian student at Columbia describes "the push and pull I felt from the African-American community—I'd meet these people wearing rasta braids, all rah-rah about Africa and talking about how we were brothers, but our cultures are totally opposite. We are very family-centered, community-centered, very religious peoples. Family is everything to us. There are no broken homes. Girls are not promiscuous. At first I felt pressure to hang around with black students and join the Black Students Society and then I realized I fit in there even less than I did with other students."

In addition to racial difference, Sinedu was further isolated by being a poor student in a very rich school—a complaint frequently voiced by the few poor students who find themselves at Harvard. The Harvard student body is diverse in many respects, but social class is not one of them. Although the admissions office likes to publicize the high proportion of students who receive some form of financial aid from the college, the figure is misleading. Most of the students on financial aid come from families who have what sociologists refer to as "cultural capital"—that is, educated families whose parents' small incomes are due to the fact that they are artists, ministers, or teachers—not blue-collar workers.

Sergio Camacho, a Mexican-American student—the son of a single uneducated mother who supported him on welfare and odd jobs throughout his childhood—says he "never remembers feeling badly about being poor until he went to Harvard. Where I was growing up everyone was poor and the ones who aren't were just a little bit better—like they were on food stamps instead of welfare. But most of the other minorities at Harvard came from fancy prep schools and knew how to blend in."

During his first year at Harvard, Sergio says, he felt "physically sick at the ostentation of the wealth. The guys that lived next door would joke about how much they were getting from their parents—

their expectations for Christmas presents. One was going to get a Land Rover if he had a B average. They would plan ski trips over winter break and go away for spring break. The guys were astonished that I didn't know how to tie a tie—I had never had one. One time our dorm was supposed to go see the dean of students to make a presentation and our proctor wanted us all to put on jackets and ties to look especially good. I told him I didn't have one, and he wouldn't let me go. I could see how Sinedu felt very lost."

The foreign students—particularly those from third-world countries—are ordinarily culled from the ruling classes in their countries and are thus often the very richest of Harvard students. Shugu Imam, the daughter of a prominent Pakistani family (her mother was the Pakistani ambassador to the United States), recalls Sinedu from a group they both participated in during their freshman year, run by a Harvard counselor, the subject of which was relating to strangers. (Shugu had halfheartedly agreed to participate in the group because the counselor was a family friend.)

"Sinedu is the only one I remember," Shugu says, "which is interesting because she wasn't very interesting. But I understood her—I thought I understood her problems more clearly than she did. I'm not surprised she didn't have any friends. She was not a compelling personality. She was completely ordinary-looking. She didn't dress well. She kept her hair tied in a bun, she wore brown—she was small, of average weight, everything about her looked average. I had no sense of her as an attractive woman—I couldn't imagine men being in love with her. I never bumped into her at parties, only at the library. This group was this artificial environment where you had to listen to everyone no matter how dull their angst was. The group gave you a window into people, but the window into Sinedu wasn't that interesting. I felt for her in the way that you feel for lonely studious students, but I didn't want to befriend her. She was a geek."

When I inquire why Sinedu couldn't have made friends with other studious students, Shugu says, "Because of her Africanness, I suppose. She seemed starved to talk about Ethiopia. She would talk a lot about Ethiopian customs—how she had been the shining star of her high school and there was a lot of expectation upon her. When you're a foreign student, you have to come to terms with the fact that people aren't interested in your culture. People think of Ethiopia as a place people starve to death—that's it. You have to package it in an interesting way for them—to tell them little tidbits. You have to learn American politics—to read *Vanity Fair*. The African friends I had who were socially successful were well traveled, from fabulously wealthy or glamorous backgrounds, and the women were pretty and knew how to exoticize themselves. Sinedu seemed to be only in America for an education.

"Harvard certainly doesn't pave the way for foreign students though," she adds. "You get a two-hour orientation and that's it—at Yale you have a two-day orientation and you're told how to get around and buy clothes. There is no international students' house— Harvard discourages it because the idea is we are meant to assimilate." While foreign students are all assigned to host families, Shugu says, "the assignments are totally nominal. My host family sent me two postcards the entire year." She thinks that "Harvard is very complacent, very arrogant—there is this attitude: we're the best university on earth and you should be happy here. For someone with a fragile sense of self—I can see how it could destroy you."

There is an international students' office, but its primary function is to help the foreign scholars and visiting faculty with day care and work permits. As for undergraduates, "we don't want to segregate them," an administrator explains. "They are supposed to fit in with other students. They were examined and admitted by the same criteria."

Bethlehem Gelaw, a high school classmate of Sinedu's and a medical student at the University of Pennsylvania, describes the metamorphosis she underwent to fit into American collegiate social life. Like Sinedu, she had been quiet and studious in high school, but at college she discovered that this style didn't work. The social breakthrough for her came when she was in a fashion show; after that, people began to pay attention to her. "In Ethiopia girls are not supposed to be sexy; they are supposed to be modest," she said. "In American colleges there is so much emphasis on physical appearance."

Bethlehem explains how, when she walked through campus, her companions would be impressed as acquaintances greeted her, remarking, "Oh, you know a lot of people." She figured out that in America it was important to have numbers of friends, whereas in Ethiopia one is supposed to have a few well-chosen friends.

After the murder/suicide, newspaper accounts reported students recalling Sinedu as looking downward and not making "eye contact," as evidence of her emotional instability. But, Bethlehem explains, that's the way Ethiopian girls are *supposed* to be. *Yilugnita*—the Amharic word for the polite reserve inbred into Ethiopians, especially females—is a quality which proves singularly maladaptive in America. "In Ethiopia you are not supposed to draw attention to yourself," Bethlehem says. "In this country you really have to sell yourself— you have to stand out—to try to attract people in the way you wouldn't in Ethiopia. In Ethiopia it's very rare for people to talk about themselves. In this country unless you talk about yourself who is going to?"

Self-assertion is a quality required in many aspects of American life. Tsegaye Arrefe, an Ethiopian immigrant, recalls a pivotal experience in which, as part of a job interview, he was asked to list his good qualities and assign them numerical value. The question, Tsegaye recalls, was followed by a stunned silence on his part: how could he rate himself without immodesty? His silence cost him the job, and he realized, he says, at that moment how profoundly he would have to change if he wanted to succeed in America.

"Here you have to be forward and honest and express yourself," Bethlehem says. "People talk about very personal things—things you would never talk about in Ethiopia." The aggressively self-analytic, confessional style—the exchange of self-revelation as the basis of American friendship—is a cultural discourse Ethiopians find difficult to participate in. Another Ethiopian student described it this way: "I had once seen a Woody Allen movie and when I came here I saw people actually talked like that. The first day of freshman year, my roommates stayed up all night and talked about sexual relations. I felt very uncomfortable."

But, echoing Shugu Imam's sentiments, Bethlehem says, "I don't know if Sinedu wanted to adapt socially. In high school, she only cared about schoolwork."

Sinedu had always had good grades instead of a social life, but at Harvard, for the first time in her life, she was not ranked at the top of her class. Good American high schools try to train students in critical thinking, but Sinedu had excelled in a system that prized memorization and rote learning, using textbooks many of which dated back to the fifties. Neb Tilahun says that he recalls the shock when he first came to Harvard and had to start writing papers that required an original point of view—but he discovered it was something he actually enjoyed. Sinedu, however, was bewildered by the requirement: "Copying from one text is plaigerysm [sic] while copying from different (several) sources is RESEARCH," she wrote in a note to herself.

Her natural abilities are difficult to gauge. She had worked terribly hard in high school in order to be second in her class of thirty-two in a school to which admission—with the exception of the Ethiopian scholarship students—was not competitive and where the other students had a range of academic abilities. She had not had the experience that many of her Harvard classmates had of successfully competing in high schools with student bodies of thousands. At Harvard she found herself in premed classes of hundreds, struggling for B minuses and worrying about medical school admissions. "I need some dumm [sic] people in order to make me feel smart," she wrote in one of her notebooks.

Sinedu's junior year, her academic adviser, the master of Dunster House, Professor Karel F. Liem, told her that her grades would rule out top-tier medical schools. As Leslie Dunton-Downer put it, "Grades like that can cause serious stress. Those are going-to-medical-school-in-Mexico grades." Or not going at all. In the nineties, medical school applications around the country have been at a record high and increasing numbers of Harvard students have failed to be admitted anywhere.

"It's much more competitive to try to get into medical school from Harvard," Trang's friend Hans Stohrer says. "The realities of competition are so stark—people are driven to desperate extremes. Handouts supposed to be on reserve at the library are stolen. People note-take in pens with multiple-colored inks. The classes are silent, except for the clicking of people changing colors in their pens. You can feel the tension."

Unlike humanities classes, where grade inflation has soared, premed classes are graded on a curve so that half the class has to do badly. A famous Harvard premed story from the eighties concerns two roommates, both of whom were applying to medical schools. One asked the other to mail his applications for him. The following spring, when the student received no responses from schools, he discovered his roommate had thrown all his applications away.

Although in high school teachers like Maura McMillin understood that they could not expect Ethiopian students to talk in class the way the Americans did, in Harvard classes participation is frequently mandatory and graded. In one of a series of diaries Sinedu kept at Harvard, she describes the agonies of being forced to give a presentation in biology class. As she muddled her way through her material, groping for English words, she became paralyzed by the fear that she could not hold the attention of the class: they were bored, perhaps even laughing at her. When the next student made his presentation she saw the terrible contrast between them: suddenly the "shriveled figures" of her classmates woke up and began to smile. He had "charm," and she didn't. He made up games with which to engage the class—games she felt she could not have thought of and which, even if she had been able to—she wrote with great self-reproach—she felt she would not have had the confidence to enact.

In Bertrand Russell's autobiography he recalls how, during his student days, he used to go alone to a certain footpath across a field "to watch the sunset and contemplate suicide. I did not, however, commit suicide," he wrote, "because I wished to know more of mathematics." Although academic achievement had always been the focus of her energies, Sinedu seems to have derived no real pleasure or spiritual nourishment from intellectual life. The passage depicting the humiliation of the biology class presentation is actually one of the few entries in the whole of her voluminous diaries to mention academics. The preoccupation of Sinedu's writings is her loneliness and the question of how to solve her "social problems."

Almost all of Sinedu's journals are written in English—a choice which, in and of itself, may be part of her effort to assimilate socially in America. The act of diary-keeping is a Western one: there is no tradition of it in Ethiopia, as there is in America, where girls are frequently given diaries with little locks in elementary school. Moreover, the kinds of things Sinedu wrote about are difficult to express in Amharic. For example, one can say one is "sad" or "not happy" in Amharic, but there is no equivalent for the English word "depression" or any of the psychotherapeutic language that is part of the vernacular in our country. The passages in her diaries in Amharic are almost always the least personal—and usually take the form of footnotes or starred glosses on English passages.

Perhaps—as one of the policemen involved in the case suggested—Sinedu wanted the record of her struggles to be understood by Americans. (In college I was so fearful my roommates would read my diaries that I wrote certain passages in Ecclesiastical Latin, which I was studying at the time—passages now rendered incomprehensible to me.)

Reading someone else's diaries is a disorienting experience. It is difficult to know how to interpret a diary, what the norms are. (What, for example, would someone gather from my own diaries? That I can't get along with any of the people I'm closest to?) Opening Sinedu's diaries for the first time, I felt a profound sense of unease. I obtained access to her journals six months after Sinedu's death through a Public Records Act Claim because the office that handles such claims had made the determination that the case records should be public—that in murdering Trang Sinedu committed a public act and changed from a girl with private problems to the subject of an investigation. Had Sinedu lived, of course, there would have been a trial, in which Sinedu's diaries would have been crucial evidence in exploring questions of motive and state of mind. But because she died the police work was limited to determining what—literally—happened, and the physical evidence was such that that was easily done.

But Sinedu's story seems to have been one she wanted to tell. She planned her death carefully and she left her diaries in a place where they might easily be found. She also sent cassette tapes and some journal writings to the woman in California whom she met through a news group on the Internet. I hadn't admitted her to my class because the writing she had submitted was boring. But her journals display uncanny capacities for self-expression and self-analysis. She left behind an extraordinary record: that of an intelligent, insightful, strong-willed person using all those capacities to fight as hard as she could for mental health—and losing, day by day, hour by hour.

Many of Sinedu's diaries take the form of spiral-bound notebooks, entitled: "My Small Book of Social Rules," "The Social Problems I Faced," "Wisdom," "Amazing Improved Events and How I Could Have Solved Them," "Set Your Priorities," "2d Quarter," "There Are Some Strict," "Depression," and "Stress." These notebooks consist primarily of hundreds of meticulous numbered instructions—sometimes in a Q and A format—in which she tries to set down the rules of American social life.

On the first page of her notebook, "Wisdom," Sinedu explains that "there are some strict rules" that govern social life and it is necessary to figure these out "as tools to manipulate your social life." The language with which she writes is odd, obsessive, and at moments imaginative, the deviations from standard written English too numerous to "[sic]." She often addresses herself in the second or third person—referring to herself as "Baby,"—creating a kind of split between her lonely naive Ethiopian self and an analytical teacherly self, who is alternately babying and berating. She also made cassette tapes with hours and hours of the same kind of minute self-analysis.

Many of Sinedu's rules concern manners. She records lessons in American table manners (Ethiopians eat with their hands), harshly scolding herself for a lapse at a dinner party when she forgot to put her napkin on her lap, telling herself everyone must have thought she was a barbarian. "I bet they've noticed," she wrote. "Yours was the only one left in the cup." In one entry she instructs herself not to eat when she is having a meal with other people because she can eat any time and the important thing is to try to engage others in conversation. But in a later entry she revises the rule, deciding that she *should* eat after all because otherwise the others will feel "greedy & jungle-like." She reminds herself to look straight into the eyes of a person who is talking to you, as is proper in America, so that people will know she is interested in continuing the conversation. She counsels herself not to fantasize excessively about who her ideal friend might be, but to be open to anyone who might like her.

She resolves that "the biggest goal" in her life should be to "make people like you," to be a "fresh pink rose in a sunny garden," because "nobody hates that, everyone wants to have it."

"I am tired of being boring," she wrote, "I would like to be a lollipop people would like to have more and more of, not a cooked asparagus." The three things she writes that she most wants to convey about herself are: "1. You're somebody. 2. You're interesting. 3. You're easy to be with, no awkwardness involved."

Above all, she resolves, she must try to *appear* normal. She urges herself: "Do not show off what you really think. Put on a mask. If you are talking about something serious, make your face serious. If you want to threaten, put away your smile and look ominous. . . ." She begs herself to learn the art of false merriment, instructing herself to laugh "falsely" regardless of her feelings, and smile at appropriate moments.

What constitutes a normal response to others is a question Sinedu finds baffling. She writes of one incident in which Neb began talking about a forthcoming school dance, telling her how beautiful she would look if she had a beautiful dress and hairstyle and makeup. The complimentary, flirtatious banter—even from an old friend—left her at a loss: she could feel herself glaring at him, with "annoyance" and a "dead" expression. She knew she should have said something "playful," she writes: "But what? What kind of words, tone. . . ?"

Her "GREATEST" problem, Sinedu decides, is figuring out what people talk about with each other—a problem she resolves to master by treating it as if it were homework for a rigorous extra course. Every morning, she decides, she should wake up at 7:45 A.M., pray, and then come up with three "fat" topics of conversation. She knows how difficult this could be, she writes, but there is no reason that she should not put the effort into this that she puts into her classes. When she has composed her topics, she writes, she should give herself a grade for them.

She tells herself that conversation should be upbeat, never negative or critical of the other person or anything they hold dear like food or culture. She should try to engage others, she writes, by asking personal questions and avoiding general topics like the weather. When she first came to the United States, Sinedu had been struck by the fact that, unlike in Ethiopia—where there are only two seasons during which the weather is the same every day—in America the weather is a frequent source of conversational commentary and speculation. But later in her diaries Sinedu figures out that talking about the weather isn't the kind of conversation that brings you closer to others. Yet the sort of conversation that does advance intimacy remains elusive to her.

All of Sinedu's rules have a doomed autistic-like quality—doomed because, as those who suffer from autism often know, human interaction is too complex for mimicry. A friend told me a story about an autistic man he knows who had learned that a girlfriend is a woman you have sex with. So he went to a bar—a place, he had been told, where men can meet women—and went up to a woman and said, "Will you be my girlfriend and have sex with me?" Bewildered as to why this approach was so unsuccessful, the autistic man sought advice again and had it explained that you can't just ask someone to have sex with you—you have to joke with them first, get to know them. So the man tried again, going up to a woman, telling a joke, and then asking about the sex.

Those who lack basic abilities to relate to others find those qualities impossible to fake because people respond to a myriad of conscious and unconscious verbal and nonverbal signals from one another. People found Sinedu boring because they felt no emotional engagement with her—an absence of a response characteristic of people suffering from all types of mental illness. A schizophrenic man describes his sense of mummification: "It is as if there is a layer of cotton wool between me and the world I can never get out of. Through it I can't hear or talk to people right." Sylvia Plath describes the hermetic quality of depression in which no matter where she is, she remains "sitting under the same glass bell jar, stewing in my own sour air." Another woman struggling with mental illness describes her feeling of difference as being "like I'm missing thumbs or something." An autistic woman profiled by Oliver Sacks describes her relation to humanity as resembling that of an anthropologist on Mars. Even in early childhood, Sinedu writes, she had some "clues of being on the outside of society. It felt as if the other girls had some kind of sixth sense that I was foreign to."

The names of at least thirty other students are mentioned in Sinedu's diaries, but they appear in a disconnected, interchangeable fashion. She has an intellectual understanding of the concept of empathy, and many of her rules concern trying to cultivate it: to try to figure out what the other person is interested in, to ask them questions about it, and to try to imagine herself in the other person's position, and so forth. But she seems utterly unable to feel it.

She describes the terrible feelings of dissociation: what she calls "this heart-failer thing"—how at some point in a conversation the thread gets lost and she "stops caring." She feels "dead and it is hard to warm myself up." She also writes that she often finds she has difficulty listening because she is so consumed by the anxiety of formulating an appropriate response.

She knows that, while one element of intimacy involves trying to enter the other's world, the other involves opening oneself up. She tells herself that when people ask her how she is doing she should not just respond, "Okay," but rather try to gauge from their expression or the length of their inquiry how interested they are in her answer, and if they reveal moderate interest, proceed with some bit of personal information.

Self-revelation, however, is a subject about which she is deeply conflicted. She continually writes about the fear that were she to expose herself—her needs, her loneliness, her envy, and her aggression—others would ridicule, exploit, or destroy her. She should present herself as powerful and confident, and when she speaks about herself she must never reveal her insecurities. When she talks about how she dresses or eats or does things, she should not "grimace" lest she "dishonor" herself. She admonishes herself to avoid an entreating tone of voice and tells herself that it is better to be alone for twenty-four hours than to allow others to drag her around wherever they want to go. She must never, ever let on her desperation or others will feel superior, gloat at her patheticness, and expect her to "grovel." At every point she must guard her back and watch that she not become "the butt" of people's jokes or let others "cross that boundary." If she allows herself to show others how she really feels about them, they will "attack and hate and defend [sic] you."

"Watch out!" she warns herself. "Watch out!"

These admonitions, however, place her in a double bind: if she doesn't reveal her problems, how can anyone help her with them? In a visit to her brother Seiffe, at Dartmouth, she describes a moment in which her defenses broke down. Throughout the visit, he kept complaining that she was interfering with his ability to study. She was hurt he wasn't that interested in spending time with her. When, out of pride, she finally said she would go back to Harvard, he looked visibly relieved, and she began to cry. She writes that he softened some at her tears and asked how she would spend the remainder of the weekend in Boston. She said she would watch television. He asked if she didn't have any friends she could spend time with, and she hesitated and then said, simply, "No." She writes how she wishes to "illude [sic] to myself as reaping friends like wheat (ha ha)" and hated to reveal "the image of a lonely girl, but I know that is the truth. . . . There is no power that lies in me that I could use however I want to. I am unable to make friends. There is no magic I control."

Her attempt at self-cure had failed. The rule books and the tapes weren't working. She could not help herself, she realized, because the problem of isolation is—by definition—one that cannot be solved alone.

Though summer after freshman year, Sinedu was working in a lab and living with her cousin's family in Brookline. Although she had lived with her cousins the summer before freshman year, and had spent occasional holidays with them, she never felt close to them (as, indeed, her cousin told me when I interviewed him). It is an odd psychic construct—one on which psychotherapy depends—that people sometimes find it easier to reveal themselves to strangers. Sinedu alighted on a radical, public format to puncture her isolation: she wrote a long letter about herself and mailed copies of it to strangers whose names she picked out of the telephone directory, as well as posting a version on the Internet. She begins by explaining that she is an eighteen-year-old freshman at Harvard University, a premed majoring in biology, and that she is from Ethiopia. It is an astonishing document.

> Well, why am I writing this letter? Because I am desperate. Most of my days are long and boring that I drag through them with sigh after sigh. Even the days that I call happy are randomly pierced with pain, realizing that I am laughing standing on thin air. My problem is that I am not bonding with people. I do not make friends not even with my relatives. . . . I live in my own shell, afraid to reveal my personality and to express my opinions. Although it took me a long time to realize, I am very shy. I blush at every little thing. . . .
>
> The mention of Harvard might make you think, OK she is one of those successful people who made it in life. Unfortunately, I don't feel one tiny bit of the success. Despite the outward glory, I live in pain. All my life I have been plagued with social problems. All my life I have been wondering why I were not as happy or content as even the poorest or the stupidest girls that I have met in my life. I always felt insecure

and lonely, especially ever since my father was sent to prison for two years. Starting from that time we were becoming financially poorer and poorer. . . .

As far as I can remember my life has been hellish. . . . Year after year, I became lonelier and lonelier. I see friends deserting me. They would take every chance to show me that they did not have any love or respect for me. They made me sit by myself when we went for long school trips. I stared out the window while they had fun sitting together. I had to swallow my pride to start talking to them to prevent pitying looks from other students. All this time I was becoming an outstanding student and one not many people knew. High School turned out even worse. I got a scholarship to the best school in the country where the children of the very rich went in a country where the rich & poor could be told apart at one crazy glance. Day in and day out, I cried my head off; I was so lonely. If I went early or left late I would be roaming the yard and deserted hallways alone while other students roared with laughter and talked their hearts out standing in groups. Home was not a comforting place. I swallowed my pain and anguish just as my siblings did to theirs. I was so lonely. But I hung on tight because I wanted to come to the States in hope of a solution. The only way I could do it was through academic excellence, to get scholarship. So I made the best use of my empty days. . . .

Now I don't care about the past. . . . [But] if I live, I want to be out there in the world. Just like those my age, I want to have friends, eat with friends, spend hours on the telephone, go to parties, and if ever possible, have boyfriends. But I find it so hard. When I am with a group of people, I keep so quiet (I have nothing to say) that I send chills through those who notice me. Then I cry when people forget about me, or dislike being with me. When I am with one person, I shake with nervousness fearing that we will run out of things to say and she or he will be bored. For math I had a teacher; for painting I had a teacher; for social life I had no one. . . .

I write a lot of diaries, I make a cassette recorder listen to my problems, I recite meaningful sayings to give me encouragement, I probe deep into myself to solve emotional pains I go through, I meditate to keep myself stable. . . . I read true stories in search of solutions & so on & so forth. I don't want to give up & this year I will try harder making use of all the help I can get. . . . The one help I believe and have always believed would be very crucial for my success is someone who will constantly check in on me & share both the good and bad part of my life with me . . . one ordinary person who will invite me for jogging or taking a walk, for shopping, for watching TV together, for having dinner together a few times, etc. In these petty, but constant activities, the tips about living that I would pick up, the skills that I would develop and the peace of mind that I would get are immeasurable. After all a pat on the back means a whole lot more than a recorder that squeaks when it is done. . . .

I am like a person who can't swim chocking [sic] for life in a river. You are one of the very few people who see me struggle. . . . All you have to do is give me a hand and put into words what you already know. No expenses are involved & there are no risks. I am sure one of your concerns, if you have gotten this far in the letter is, what if I am one of those criminals lurking around. But believe me, right now I am not strong enough. I would have been aggressive rather than shy if I was to hurt others. Also, if I had no control over myself, I would not have made it to Harvard all the way from Ethiopia. . . .

All it takes is a few hours from your week and some energy. Me, I have nothing to lose. I am so desperate; please do not close the door in my face. Even if you are not interested, please give this letter to a friend or relative who might be. I would be forever grateful to hear from you.

I anxiously wait to hear from you.

This version—which appeared on a news group on the Internet—was read by a woman in California, who asked to remain anonymous. "When I read the letter, I thought it was a little spooky," she said, but she decided to answer, and they corresponded. But then Sinedu sent her "this weird cassette tape and these weird journal writings. I kind of freaked out. The thing that was so weird about it was none of them had anything to do with me—it was just her writing and talking into a tape recorder about herself. I didn't know why she sent it to me, or what she wanted from me. I never wrote back and she never contacted me again either."

One of the people who received a version of this letter in the mail was Mary Beth Johnson, a product manager at a Boston computer company. In the version Mary Beth received, Sinedu explained that she had picked her name randomly out of the Brookline phone directory. Mary Beth Johnson puzzled and puzzled over why Sinedu had selected her. She wondered if it was because of her name, which she describes as "as whitebread as you can get," and somewhat unusual in the Jewish section of Brookline where she lives. The letter had been typed and the name and address on the letter sent to Mary Beth had been laser printed on a label, "a detail," she says, "which freaked me out because it made it seem like a form letter—and made me wonder how many other people she sent it to." (Indeed, Mary Beth is one of the people I happened to find who received the letter, but Sinedu may well have sent it to dozens of others.)

As it happened, Mary Beth knew an administrator, Gayle Muello, at Harvard Law School, so she sent her the letter and asked her to do something with it. Gayle found the letter very disturbing and spent a morning making calls, trying to track down the appropriate person in the college to notify about it. She doesn't recall whom she reached and sent the letter to, but police reports note that the letter was sent to the freshman dean's office where it was read by a dean and sent on to Dunster House, where Sinedu would be living in the fall, and it was placed in her file.

The letter is revealing of Sinedu's unsuccessful interactions with the world. While she might have found it easier to reach out to strangers, there was no reason for strangers to respond to her. As Mary Beth Johnson put it, "she knew nothing about me, whether I was old or young, whether we'd have anything in common, whether I wanted new friends." She also found the tone of the letter offputting. "It was so demanding," she said, "I almost resented it. It wasn't like she wanted my help; it was like she was telling me what to do." Beneath the piteousness, she sensed aggression—the kind of plea which turns to rage at refusal (perhaps a quality I myself sensed when I was not drawn to help her take my class).

"When I read about Trang's death," Mary Beth said, "for a moment I thought, Geez, maybe I could have helped her, but then I realized: this is what happened to someone who tried."

Although Sinedu had never been close to her freshman roommate, Anna, she had nevertheless assumed that they would be living together again. It was not until just before housing decisions were due that Anna mentioned she had chosen a new roommate for sophomore year. "Damn you, you bitch!" Sinedu wrote in her diary with fury, saying that she would never forgive her, for Anna had "pranked over [her] prostrated body." She resolved to someday make Anna regret her decision.

As it happened, though, the rejection led to what Sinedu saw as her first piece of great good luck at college: Trang Ho, whom she had met in a science class, unexpectedly agreed to live with her. There had been tension between Trang and her own freshman roommate because the roommate's boyfriend slept over—a practice of which Trang disapproved. After Trang agreed to live with her, Sinedu writes in her diary, she enjoyed four days that were the "highlight" of her life at Harvard. She says she felt for the first time what it is like to be happy: she could feel her face brightening, her skin healing, her energy surging all because

> . . . my rooming problem was solved in the best possi-
> ble way saving my face and also with a girl I thought I would
> really enjoy to be with, with a girl I would make the queen of
> my life. I could just see myself raising my head proudly
> whenever people ask me who I'm rooming with.

She is filled with energy and optimism; she will work hard so as not to "spoil the beautiful chance" she has been given. "I guess the main problem of my life is going to be solved . . ." she concludes, though adding that the only thing she fears is that "shitty cringing feeling" should the rooming arrangement not work out in a way that would make her hold her "head high and speak of it proudly."

Trang's experience at Harvard had been quite different from Sinedu's. Trang's sister Thao recalls Trang as having had a difficult freshman year—struggling to find herself, academically and socially, and dealing with her parents' divorce—but by sophomore year she had found her feet. When her academic adviser, Professor Karel Liem, informed her—just as he had informed Sinedu—that her B plus grade average was not going to qualify her for top medical schools like Harvard, she told him cheerfully that it was all right. She was just happy, she said, that she had gotten into a good lab where she had the opportunity to do research.

A coworker at the lab, Todd Milne, with whom she copublished an article in *Genetics* magazine recalls that, "although she was juggling an incredible number of things, she didn't seem unduly stressed about her grades." He says she always wanted their work at the lab to be more relevant. "How does this advance medicine or relate to cancer?" she would ask. Another coworker, John Donovan, remembers how she would go around each morning and say hi to everyone in the lab, and then, at the end of the day, go around again and say good night. "That's what she was like," he said, "very sweet and thoughtful, always very cheerful, centered and driven, just a totally friendly individual."

Trang's life initially dovetailed with her new roommate's in many ways. They took the same premed classes and were often seen in the Dunster House dining hall eating together. Trang took Sinedu as her guest to her lab's Christmas party. Trang's sister, who recalls Sinedu as "very quiet," says that "for a while Sinedu and Trang were doing a lot of things together." She recalls how Sinedu used to take Trang to the Addis Red Sea Ethiopian restaurant in Boston and how, "in the beginning, things were so promising. But as time went on Trang had obligation to own self and not have that much time."

Trang had no idea that Sinedu had told her father that she was her best friend.

A lthough Sinedu had chosen Trang as her best friend, she was aware that the relationship was not reciprocal. She was jealous of Trang's life and often brooded over the imbalances between them. Trang was both doing better than she academically *and* she had a social life. While the Vietnamese Students Association provided Trang with a large community, the African Students Association had only a few Ethiopians.

In addition, Trang had a best friend—Thao Nguyen (the same first name as Trang's sister), a teacher in Lowell, Massachusetts, whom she spoke to on the phone every day. Although Sinedu tried to encourage herself to be reasonable, noting in her rule book that "you don't have to own a person totally to be their friend," she struggled with her jealousy of Thao, neglecting at times to give Trang her phone messages.

The thing Sinedu was most jealous of, however, was Trang's relationship with her family. In her journals Sinedu complains bitterly that Trang went home every Saturday and Sunday and that on many other days her sisters would "call her crying," and she would immediately pack her bags and go. Sinedu particularly suffered during school breaks, when she would often stay alone in the dorm. The heat was turned down, the dining hall closed, and all the other students were gone. Trang's sister recalls how Trang would occasionally ask her to bring a rice dish for Sinedu, but she would never invite Sinedu to go home with them. The leitmotif of an empty room is one Sinedu returns to again and again in her writings.

Even Shugu Imam recalls the shock she had felt freshman year at finding herself alone for the first time. "Before I came to Harvard," she says, "I had never slept alone in a place before. In Pakistan, there are always people around. If nothing else, there are always servants."

Even more painful to Sinedu than being alone, however, were times when Trang would have friends over. They would hang out laughing and talking in the next room, while Sinedu sat alone, pretending to study and garnering grievance. It was the situation, somehow, she had been in all her life—the laughter sounding to her like everything that had been denied her, all the joy and communion of life from which she was mysteriously permanently excluded.

Pages and pages of Sinedu's diaries are devoted to the question of how to deal with this problem. While she can't make Trang's friends talk to her, she writes, as long as they are coming into her room they should ask her permission as well as Trang's. But she is at a loss as to how to make them treat her the way she wants. She could "rank [sic] grunt and crash doors," but it would probably be futile because no one cares how she feels, she would risk a bad name for herself and possibly incur their hatred. She concludes she may be in too weak a position to take any action at all, although she thinks the incident is a "test" of her strength, and adds, "Maybe you want people to know you're there, even in hatred."

She decides she can at least try to recoup her "power" in relation to Trang. In one rule, she declares that if Trang borrows her science textbooks, then in return she, Sinedu, has a right to use anything Trang owns freely and that, if Trang "grunts" about it, Sinedu should remind her that whatever she is using is equal to the cost of Sinedu's books. In another rule, she decides perhaps she shouldn't lend her any textbooks at all. Trang's sister recalls Trang telling her how Sinedu would ask to borrow Trang's notes in their science classes, but Sinedu wouldn't share anything in return.

T rang and Sinedu's suite, H-21, consisted of two small dark low-ceilinged rooms with white stucco walls. With their small windows, massive old oak school desks, and blue and white ceramic tiled bathrooms, the rooms have a girlish, nested, old-fashioned feel—somewhere between cozy and claustrophobic. Like all the Dunster House doubles, the rooms had originally been built as a suite for one. Every time Trang wanted to go out, she had to walk through Sinedu's room, and every time Sinedu wanted to go to the bathroom, she had to walk through Trang's. It was a situation suitable for lovers or twins—for the relationship Sinedu dreamed of—not the one they had. When the relationship fractured, the setup became unbearable.

Although at the end of their sophomore year Trang had reluctantly agreed to live with Sinedu a second year, when junior year began she immediately began to regret it. Sinedu, who had previously been compulsively neat, became aggressively messy—a classic symptom of many mental disorders, including clinical depression. Though Trang had never been especially neat herself, she found their living space intolerable. She told her sister about it, but Thao couldn't imagine that neatness could be that much of a problem until she came to see it herself and was shocked. There were dirty clothes strewn about and rotting fruit. Sinedu had hung a curtain between their two rooms with the printed side of the cloth facing her own, the dull side to Trang's.

Diep Nguyen, Trang's friend, recalls how Trang "never confronted Sinedu with the problems in their relationship—she kept it all to herself. That's the Vietnamese way." Trang went to talk to the administration at Dunster House about getting a new room for spring semester, but the request was denied. Trang's sister remembers how "Sinedu was asking why are you moving, Trang didn't want to say, just hinting, but then she was denied and decided to stay." Trang's mother and sister offered to go talk to officials for her, but Trang decided she would wait out the year. Trang's sister recalls that Sinedu would sometimes call their home in Medford, asking for Trang at times when Trang was actually at school. She would feel awkward, knowing that Trang must have been avoiding going back to her room.

Thao Nguyen recalls that "things got uglier the second semester. Sinedu wouldn't let go; Trang kept feeling bad." In April, Trang asked two other girls to room with her the following year, and they agreed. Depression often causes regression—feelings of extreme childlike dependency. Trang's withdrawl seems to have triggered feelings of depression in Sinedu which made her all the more dependent on Trang. First Assistant District Attorney Martin Murphy believes that "Trang became much more important to Sinedu *after* she rejected her."

When Trang told Sinedu about her decision, Sinedu followed her out of their suite and onto the subway, begging her to change her mind. Trang recoiled; she told Thao she felt Sinedu's pleading revealed a lack of self-esteem. And Sinedu's living habits, Trang told Thao, showed "Sinedu didn't respect herself." But Trang felt anxious about the decision. Whenever Trang thought she was hurting someone she would go to Thao and say, "Am I a bad girl? Am I ugly?" and Thao would reassure her, as she did now, telling her that it was all right to change roommates.

Sinedu decided to approach the girls Trang was going to room with, and ask whether she could join their group. Initially they agreed, but then they told Trang and Trang said no—she had asked to live with them in order to get *away* from Sinedu.

Sinedu then wrote Trang a letter in which she begged her to reconsider. Trang showed the letter to her sister, who found it peculiar. Sinedu wrote how glad she was that they had become friends, and how much fun they had had together. Then she said that Trang was very mean not to have spent much time with her that year and not to room with her again. "I thought we were going to do stuff together," she wrote. "You'll always have your family to go to and I am going to have no one"—a quote which after the murder became a *Newsweek* "Perspectives" quote of the week. She ended the letter by telling Trang that if she changed her mind about their friendship to give her call—a sentiment Thao found odd as they lived together.

Trang wrote back, trying to mollify her, using words like "respect," which she knew would make sense to Sinedu:

> Sinedu,
>
> As I told you, I have no resentment towards you. It's just our living habits are different. I don't want to belabor this point. It's unfair of you to accuse me of causing you unhappiness about rooming. Come to think of it, I have been very tolerant and as nice as possible to you. I respect you so you should respect my decision. Furthermore, your actions about what happened really hurt me. If I had neither care nor think of you as a friend, it would not have hurt me. I am really sorry that I have not been around much to "hang out," with you. Despite what happened, I hope we can still be friends.
>
> T

Sinedu was left "to float"—to be randomly paired with a roommate by the Dunster House office. In a school where most people choose their roommates, especially by their senior year, there is a sense of failure associated with floating: the stigma that no one wants to live with you. An editorial written by a Harvard student stated that he understood how Sinedu felt, for floating was worse than death. As Leslie Dunton-Downer put it, "To float for your senior year—to suddenly face the possibility of being stuck in a room with random sophomores who can't find Ethiopia on a map—that's a tough thing." In another house, Sinedu might have simply requested a single, but Dunster *has* only doubles—a situation which causes problems because a certain number of students can't get along with any roommate.

R oommates are not often included on the map of primal human relationships, but they can have great emotional significance—as a kind of makeshift family, way stations between the households of childhood and adulthood. After the rejection, Sinedu and Trang stopped speaking. Once when Trang forgot her keys, Sinedu refused to let her in and Trang had to call a security guard, who harassed her for not having ID. Trang felt humiliated when the guard opened the door and saw her roommate sitting on her bed.

Instead of strengthening her other relationships that spring, Sinedu withdrew from everyone. When Neb called her, she put him off so often that he finally asked if he had offended her in some way. She told him she was just busy with organic chemistry. In fact, she wasn't spending her time studying: according to some teachers, she was "in dire straits" in some of her science courses. Neb said he would leave it up to her to call him, and he didn't hear from her again until the end of the semester. She told him nothing about the rooming decision. She told her cousins that *she* had instigated the break with Trang, but she had wanted to live with these other girls, and Trang had turned them against her.

The slight is an important concept in Ethiopian culture. Ethiopians say they are often struck by how Americans are always tossing off the words "Oh, I'm sorry." In Ethiopia slights are grave offenses, difficult to set right. People rarely attempt to apologize directly to each other, but instead negotiate through a third person—often an elder. The ancient tradition of revenge—*tikat*, or bloodletting—still exists in the countryside: a Capulet and Montague tradition which can be responsible for the annihilation of entire families.

Trang had insulted and disappointed Sinedu. Sinedu returned to a plan she had first penned in her diary in the fall of their sophomore year. The entry begins: "On the way to depression and battered w/ pessimistic thoughts. I am saying there is no use to my life. I am unlovable and a cuckoo. . . . Trang told me I am boring. I felt like I'm boring her. . . ." Then she has a moment of insight: she bores Trang because of her own lack of emotional capacities. Trang has a family and "knows what warmth is, & tries to get it from me," but she is unable to respond to Trang because she has "no one I trust & no one I miss & so I know no warmth. . . ."

The despair this realization engenders seems to turn immediately to rage, which she channels toward a new object, writing: "I hate Adey. If I ever grow desperate enough to seek power & fearful respect through killing, she will be the 1st one I would blow off. . . . The way she acts, she acts as if I am no more importance than a crawling insect."

What makes her feel the most hopeless, she writes, is the sense that the situation will never "reverse": others will continue on, "tucked" in their rich full lives, and she will "cry alone in the cold." And "the hopelessness of change," the knowledge that she "can't return the evil, kills the life of me." She concludes:

> The bad way out I see is suicide & the good way out killing, savoring their fear & then suicide. But you know what annoys me the most, I do nothing. You would think I was

both hand & leg-cuffed to a couch stuck in the ground.
Sometimes even if a bomb falls beside me, I would be scared
at first and then not even bother to see what happened.

The two solutions reflect Sinedu's ambivalence about the source
of her problems. She sees the basic solution to her isolation—the one
that appears in both the good and the bad solutions—as self-annihila-
tion. But the "bad" solution, suicide, involves taking sole responsibility for her unhappiness. The "good" solution, on the other hand,
involves avenging herself against all those who rejected her.

Although Trang is mentioned in the passage, her fury focuses on
Adey Fisseha, a popular Ethiopian-American classmate. Adey was,
ironically, a member of the African Students Association who spoke
about Sinedu at the large informational meeting four days after the
deaths, and recalled Sinedu as "nice." She told me she considered
Sinedu a friend she didn't know well but with whom she was always
on cordial terms. She had no idea that in Sinedu's mind she was part
of the conspiracy of all those who had rejected her, against whom she
was planning revenge—revenge which in the spring of her junior
year came to be directed solely at Trang.

Like many people contemplating suicide, Sinedu sought help to
dissuade her from her plan. Although three separate Harvard
officials told me that Sinedu never sought help of any kind, in
fact she had been seeing a counselor at the University Health Services, Dr. Douglas Powell, since freshman year (a fact Harvard was
surprisingly successful at keeping out of the press, despite the extensive coverage of the case.) Dr. Randolph Catlin, the director of
Mental Health Service, was quoted in *Boston* magazine as speculating

that perhaps Sinedu didn't avail herself of counseling because, like many Harvard students, she might have perceived it as a sign of failure.

In a list of things "to talk to Dr. Powell" about which was found among her papers, Sinedu writes that she is concerned that she is incapable of forgiveness. If people do anything that hurts her, she writes, forever afterward when she thinks about them her heart "will go cold." How does forgiveness work? Is it that others express anger at the time, while she keeps it all inside her?

Dr. Powell tells me that he is under a "gag order" by the university but refers me to Dr. Catlin—a man I know personally and like. Speaking in general terms about the murder, Dr Catlin speculates: "The threat of the loss of the relationship with Trang obviously mattered to Sinedu very much. A strong person will react to a loss by seeking other relationships, but in order to see alternatives you need to have a good self-image, attuned to imagine yourself in a variety of situations and relationships.

"If your self-esteem is shaky and very narrowly based, such as on intellectual functioning alone, and you are really unsure of your value as a human being, it becomes terribly important to feel there is one person who cares about you. You may take a rejection as clear evidence that you as a person are not valuable, and that might make you enormously angry—so angry you can't deal with it. A primitive response is to destroy that person, or yourself or both. That way the punishment fits the crime, and you also solve the problem—you're not going to be hurt again.

"It is very rare though," he adds, "to see it acted upon in this way."

When Sinedu decided to die, she set about planning it in the same methodical fashion in which she had always conducted her life. She wrote to a relative that she had always promised them a *gabe* blanket (a finely woven blanket, given as a gesture of respect) and that she wanted to give it now. She sent her sisters in Ethiopia a present. Two weeks before the end of the semester she packed up her computer, meticulously, in its original packaging and sent it to one of her cousins. For the first time in months, she called Neb.

Neb was surprised to hear from her—the Sinedu he knew would never make plans during exam period. But he was pleased too—he had never understood the reason for her distance. Sinedu felt he shared none of her assimilatory struggles. In her diaries she expresses jealousy and competitiveness with him over what she saw as the advantages of his cosmopolitan background and outgoing personality.

They arranged to have brunch on Sunday, a week before she died. When Sinedu arrived that day, Neb was struck by the transformation in her appearance. She was wearing makeup, high patent leather heels, and shorts, "a change from her Ethiopian self where wearing shorts is considered disrespectful." It was especially striking because during exam period she usually wore sweats. Surprised, he told Sinedu she looked "spectacular." He asked after Trang and Sinedu said she was fine. She told him a guy had invited her to a formal and she had said no, but she wouldn't tell him who the person was. He felt "there was a profound change in the way she looked and moved and carried herself. There was an air of happiness about her. She seemed lighter."

It was the happiest he had ever seen her. He is certain now that she was saying good-bye. After her death he found himself particularly disturbed by the memory. But, Dr. Catlin explains, when suicidal patients finally make up their minds to die, they frequently feel better. "You often see people in mental hospitals who are extremely depressed for a long time and then suddenly they seem to be better so they get let out and then they kill themselves—and you find out later that that's what they were planning all along. You realize that the reason they became so cheerful was that they had finally solved their problem. They had settled on a plan—one which really demonstrates where they're coming from."

It is "a plan formulated as a way of dealing with an intolerable reality—the feeling of absolute aloneness. There is nothing worse than to feel one is totally alone, there is no one in the world you care about or who cares about you and therefore you have no meaning to yourself." When people are alone in the wilderness, he says, after a while they will begin to hallucinate companions, their psychic need for company is so great.

I n the following week Sinedu took one exam (for which she received an A) and then became unable to study. Students report seeing her in the library, "distracted, with a glazed look." She purchased a length of nylon rope and two large knives—a four-inch open hunting knife and a large silver kitchen knife (the sources of which were never discovered). That Tuesday she wrote Jennifer Tracy, one of the two girls Trang had chosen to room with, a letter that she never mailed, obsessing about Trang's betrayal, saying she had "had it" with her, and that the rooming incident had created so much "evil" between them that rooming with her was like "burning in hell." The letter ends with a plea for Jennifer to talk to her.

On Wednesday she missed her chemistry exam, and on Thursday her neurobiology exam. She went to the University Health Services and got medical excuses for both of them—a pattern she had established (she had a medical excuse in a previous semester as well). On Tuesday or Wednesday of that week, she dropped off a photograph of herself at *The Harvard Crimson*, the student daily newspaper, with the typed message, "KEEP this picture. There will soon be a very juicy story involving the person in this picture." On the outside of the envelope she typed "IMPORTANT."

The photo she picked didn't look much like her: it was a touched-up professional shot from high school that gives her both a glamor and a slightly sinister air which she never had. But she had accurately anticipated the way in which, when someone dies, a single photo can come to represent that person: many more people now know Sinedu from that photo than from life. Perhaps she had also noticed that the three previous suicides that spring had not been given much play in the paper and she wanted to ensure what she got: three *Crimson* issues devoted to the unfolding drama of her death.

The ability to imagine and manipulate the publicity attendant on her own death is one of the most striking aspects of the murder. It is as if Sinedu were writing the teaser to a cheap mystery. Ashwini Sukthankar says she can hear Sinedu say it: "She would use phrases like that—'a very juicy story,' 'it isn't my cup of tea'—half self-consciously, stressing every word because they weren't really natural to her. I had never even heard her swear."

The letter is a detail Ethiopians find particularly repulsive and bewildering. "It was the letter which first made many Ethiopians suspicious," said Misrak Assefa, the owner of the Addis Red Sea Ethiopian restaurant in Boston and a friend of Sinedu's cousins. Like many in the Boston Ethiopian community, she does not believe Sinedu committed the murder. "The letter is totally un-Ethiopian," she says.

The *Crimson* editors had no idea what to make of the letter. The wording wasn't calculated to inspire alarm; it seemed more like a prank than a cry for help. As it was, the letter kicked around the office for a few days and then was thrown into the dumpster, where police later recovered it.

On Friday, May 26, Thao Nguyen came to spend Memorial Day weekend with Trang. Trang was taking her final exam on Saturday and afterward Thao was to help her move home for the summer. Thao, an ethereal-looking twenty-nine-year-old, had met Trang two summers before when they were both teaching at MICAS, shortly after Thao immigrated to America.

Like Trang, Thao had endured great hardship to come to the States. In the last days of the Vietnam War her father was offered escape on an American ship, but he turned back because there wasn't time to get his family from their village. A few days later the Hanoi government announced that everyone who had fought on the side of the Americans had to turn themselves in and go to a reeducation camp for three months. Thao's father did and was kept ten years. When he got out, the family waited another five years to get visas to leave the country—during which time, by virtue of having applied for visas, the family was harassed and Thao's father denied work. By the time they immigrated, Thao was twenty-seven; she had to leave behind her teaching job, her boyfriend, and all her friends, and begin her life again.

Thao's first job in America at MICAS involved teaching students, many of whom had been in the country longer than she had, while she was struggling to learn English. (She had studied French at college in Vietnam.) One day her boss rebuked her and she didn't understand what he was saying and Trang translated for her, smoothing over the situation. After that, Trang became Thao's first friend in America, taking her shopping, showing her how things worked, insisting that they speak English between themselves to help Thao learn. That fall Thao got a job teaching immigrant children in the public schools in Lowell, Massachusetts. On weekends she would sometimes take a bus into Cambridge and stay with Trang in her dorm room.

Trang and Thao spent that Friday night packing Trang's things for the summer. At one point, Thao remembers, they came across a traditional Ethiopian dress. Trang told Thao that Sinedu had brought it for her from her trip home the previous August, and then said, a little wistfully, that all that was over now. The next morning Trang went out to study for her afternoon exam in physics—a course Sinedu was also taking. As Trang opened the door to Sinedu's room to leave, they could see Sinedu hunched on the bed, in a fetal position, her knees up, holding her head in her hands, looking down and crying. When Trang returned at noon, Sinedu was still in the same position. Thao told Trang she should ask Sinedu what was wrong. Trang felt uncomfortable, saying they hadn't talked in two months, but she opened the door and asked Sinedu if she was okay. Sinedu silently waved her away. Trang wondered if she had failed an exam, and they decided to leave her alone.

Then Trang went out to take the three-hour exam. Shortly afterward Sinedu left the room. She didn't speak to Thao before she left, but she fixed a cold blank gaze upon her. Thao assumed she had also gone to take the physics exam. Thao stayed in Trang's room reading until Trang came back at five or six. When Trang came in, she could see Sinedu was in her room again and some things had been packed. Trang said, "Wow, I'm done," and they went to the Hong Kong restaurant to celebrate with Trang's future roommate Jennifer Tracy. Trang called Hans Stohrer and left him a message inviting him to join them, but he wasn't in.

Trang hadn't seen Sinedu at the exam, but enough students were taking the exam that Sinedu would have been easy to miss. Trang had no idea that Sinedu had missed her previous two exams as well. When they were about to leave for the evening, they heard Sinedu talking and crying on the telephone to someone they assumed was her brother Seiffe. Seiffe later told a Harvard official that when he spoke to Sinedu she had said she was fine—she was only worn out from exams and had diarrhea.

No one knows exactly how Sinedu spent her last night. A Harvard security guard told the police that at 6:30 P.M. that night Sinedu had come and requested a key to her room, telling him that she had locked herself out. He had seen her throughout the year and she had always appeared lonely to him, but that night she was smiling and in a jovial mood. A little while later she returned again and asked if he would let her into the weight room, which he found unusual, as she had never made the request before and students who used the weight room knew how to get in without a key. Around 8:30 P.M. he saw her standing on the street outside Dunster House. He asked what she was doing, and she told him she was waiting for a friend to pick her up. It struck him as unusual, he told the police, that he had seen Sinedu three times in a short period of time that evening. The police were unable to locate anyone else who saw Sinedu that night or discover who, if anyone, she had been waiting for.

Trang and Thao tried to go see the movie *While You Were Sleeping,* but it was sold out, so instead they watched a video in a friend's room, about two sisters who were in love with the same guy. Thao asked Trang what she would do in such a situation, but Trang didn't see the conflict: she couldn't imagine a man being more important to her than her sister. When they got back to the room at two in the morning, Sinedu was lying on her bed, with the light on.

Trang and Thao went to bed, sharing Trang's bed as Trang did with her little sister at home. Thao was dismayed when this fact was later misinterpreted: all over Southeast Asia women share beds and are physically affectionate. Trang used to tell Thao, "We can't hold hands when we're walking down the street—we're in America now." In Vietnam it's only a problem if a girl holds hands with a boy. They talked for another hour or two that night—Thao telling Trang all about herself and her past in Vietnam, things she had never told anyone before. When Trang asked why she was so unusually talkative Thao said, "Because this is the last time we're going to see each other." Trang said, "What do you mean?" and Thao said quickly, "I meant this is the last time we're going to see each other here at school." She is afraid now that this slip of the tongue may have brought bad fortune upon Trang—or that if she told other Vietnamese people the story they would believe that she had.

After Trang closed her eyes, Thao stared at Trang's face for a long time: her skin pale with exhaustion, but relaxed, her worries drained away. Then she turned, so they could sleep head to toe in the narrow bed.

Sometime before eight in the morning an alarm went off, but Trang murmured to Thao that it was Sinedu's and to go back to sleep. Sinedu was already in the bathroom. They heard her cross through their room to turn off the alarm and then go back into the bathroom. Thao heard the sound of water running and then she fell back asleep. She awoke to see Sinedu standing over Trang, stabbing her silently with a huge knife and a fixed, glazed expression—"intent, like she really knew what she was doing." Trang was holding up her hands to try to block the knife, unable to cry out.

Thao, lying the opposite way from Trang, tried to kick at the knife but got cut in the foot. She sat up and tried to grab the blade, but Sinedu pulled it away, slicing open Thao's hand. Bleeding heavily, Thao ran out of the room. She heard the heavy self-locking door click behind her and realized, with horror, she would never be able to go back. It was the worst moment of her life. Frantically, she began banging on the other doors in the hall, but the students were all sleeping and no one opened up. She stumbled out into the courtyard, where a lone student, Lloyd Marcom, was sitting in the sun, eating his breakfast and waiting for the others to wake up. Lloyd recalls her screaming, hysterical, saying over and over, "She killed my friend." He saw that she was bleeding heavily from her hand and foot, and he took off his shirt to make a tourniquet, but she cried, "Don't help me, help my friend," so he went to the phone to call the police.

By the time he got back there was a crowd around Thao, trying to bandage her hand. The police arrived and went upstairs with their guns drawn. Thao was put into an ambulance, accompanied by police, and taken to Cambridge City Hospital. Thao kept asking about her friend and crying, "Why didn't she kill me instead?" The police assured her that her friend would be fine, and that whenever they had any information, she'd be the first to know.

Whenthe police entered H-21, as they stated in their reports, in the first bedroom—Sinedu's room—they found an: "Asian female, lying face up, feet towards the door, parallel to the bed, and in a pool of blood. Blood splattered the walls, bed and floor." The victim had "multiple wounds to her neck, chest, and arms. A check for vitals showed no respiration or heartbeat. Victim was wearing a red blouse, pulled over her naval, exposing her red bra, tan shorts. All clothing was saturated with blood."

One of the officers transmitted to control that Thao should be covered by an officer and considered in custody until her involvement could be ascertained. The officer accompanying her to the hospital was instructed to record any statements she made.

A heavy desk had been pushed against the door to the second bedroom—Trang's room—barricading it from the inside. When the officers were able to get in they found the bed and room splattered with blood. In the center of a pool of blood on the floor was an open buck knife, pointing toward the first bedroom.

Inside the bathroom they discovered a black female hanging by a rope secured to the shower curtain rod. Because the shower was old-fashioned, with a heavy pole resting on marble slats, it had held her weight. A large kitchen knife with a black handle was found in the female's left front pocket, blade point up. No stab wounds were observed on her. The officers cut her down, and a professional ambulance crew arrived on the scene and attempted to revive her, but she died soon thereafter.

It was immediately evident to the police that the third female was the perpetrator. The windows in the barricaded bedroom and bathroom were dusty and locked; she could only have been alone when she hanged herself. They could also deduce that she had set up the noose ahead of time, because the rope which was used had been cut to the right size and the rest of the coil neatly replaced in a cabinet. If the hanging had been spontaneous, she could have taken the whole coil and let the extra rope dangle.

From the fact that Trang's body was discovered in Sinedu's room, police concluded Trang had managed to get up from her bed, stumbled into the next room, sat momentarily on Sinedu's bed, and then collapsed onto the floor. Thao finds the idea that her friend had tried to walk unbearable; she is certain that Sinedu must have moved her into the other room.

The police reports record forty-five stab wounds on Trang's

body, including eleven on the chest, neck, and head area. Three stab wounds were identified as the cause of death: one through the left ventricle of the heart and two to the left lung.

"All officers filed reports on this tragic incident at Dunster House," a report concludes.

K arel Liem went to notify the Ho family of their daughter's death, accompanied by two policemen and a friend of Trang's, Huong Mai, who would translate. They drove to an address in Medford, but the family had moved, so they had to stop at a pay phone and call and ask where they lived. Trang's mother wanted to know what was happening, but Huong kept repeating, "Just stay there, we need to come see you."

When they arrived, Huong told Trang's mother and her sister Tram in Vietnamese that there had been an accident and Trang was dead. Trang's mother began to cry hysterically, screaming no, she was going to go pick her up now. She started toward the door and they had to hold her back.

The police called Trang's sister Thao, who had been spending the weekend with her boyfriend in Connecticut. Eventually, Dr. Catlin arrived from the Mental Health Service. He discovered Quy Huynh prostrate with grief on the couch, in hysterics. He knelt down and gave her a tranquilizer and put his arms around her. He had never seen loss so overwhelming before, he said.

FIVE

Looking for a Villain

In the wake of the disaster, the question everyone asked was: Could anything have been done to prevent it? As one student put it, "When all this was brewing, where were all the grown-ups? Are we alone here at college?" The incident sparked a lot of debate about the meaning of *in loco parentis*, and how to treat students as adults, while taking care of the ways that they aren't. The questions involved are complex: to what extent can a large, diversely populated institution be responsible for the welfare of its members?

They are questions, however, Harvard did not wish to have explored. The tragedy was the climax of a year with an unusual number of public relations disasters, and doubtless with the advice of some of their eleven in-house lawyers, the university adopted a policy of spin control and stonewalling. The answer to every question I asked—from whether Sinedu checked out a Japanese novel about suicide found in her suite with the bleakest passages underlined to the nature of the medical excuses for her exams (were they psychological ones?)—was "That information is confidential." Harvard employees are not supposed to talk to the press without checking with the news office—a process which kept resulting in my interviews being abruptly canceled. Harry Lewis, the dean of Harvard college, announced to faculty at an Ad Board meeting (Harvard's disciplinary board) that no one should speak to the press, in general, and especially not to *The New Yorker* reporter, whom he characterized as "particularly persistent."

Emboldened by pique, I decided to telephone Dean Fred Jewett to complain. When I ask whether he thinks stonewalling is appropriate, he says simply, "In a case of this complexity we prefer to centralize information. Everyone's looking for a villain," he adds, "and we don't want to be it." Another dean explains to me that of course they don't want outsiders investigating while Harvard is conducting its own internal review. Who will be the recipient of that review? I ask. The press? Of course not. The students? That would be inappropriate. The families? It might cause them pain.

Detective James Dwyer, who headed the Cambridge Police Department's investigation, tells me that trying to find out information from Harvard is like "trying to ask questions of this file cabinet." Harvard always wants to handle everything internally, he says; they frequently "forget" to report campus suicides and rapes to the Cambridge police: "The coroner's office calls us about a body and we say, 'What body?' It turns out there's been another suicide at Harvard and Harvard hasn't reported it. When we contact Harvard they say, 'Oh, sorry, our mistake,'" he says, "but there's a pattern of these mistakes." The Cambridge police tried interviewing some people after the murder/suicide, but "it was like dancing around on a pin" so they had to leave it to the Harvard police, who submitted their reports to the district attorney's office, which was overseeing the investigation.

The district attorney's office says that the Harvard police shared with them some, but not all, of their information. The case file at the district attorney's became publicly available (through a Public Records Act claim) but, because Harvard is a private institution, it is not required to and did not choose to make its police work available for examination. However, Assistant District Attorney Martin Murphy says that questions about Harvard's responsibility "would never be a relevant question to us because our job is only to look at the crime, and confirm that it was indeed a murder/suicide and who the killer was."

In recent years Harvard has had a good deal of crime to report. In February 1995, Charles Lee, '93 cochair of the university's Jimmy Fund, a charity that benefits children with cancer, was sentenced to one year in prison for stealing $120,000 from the fund. He was charged with having written himself more than eighty checks with the fund's money in order to finance a lifestyle his senior year, which included lavish meals, designer clothing, trips, and stereo equipment. A week later the treasurer, David Sword, pleaded guilty to having stolen nearly $7,000. In 1994, a Harvard Business School student, Daniel Young, pleaded guilty to fraud while working at Manufacturers Hanover Trust. In 1993, Christopher Garvey, a twenty-six-year-old Harvard graduate, pleaded guilty to insider trading charges. In 1991, John M. Fountain, a Harvard senior, was indicted for attempting to extort $10,000 from a Los Angeles physician by threatening to inform the media of the doctor's positive HIV status. In 1990, Kevin Watkins, a Harvard law student who had risen from the ghetto of Crown Heights, Brooklyn, was convicted of raping his former girlfriend, a Harvard undergraduate, when she went to his apartment to retrieve videotapes he had made of them having sex. In 1989, Harvard football player Jose Luis Razo, Jr.—a former Boys Club "Boy of the Year"—was sentenced to ten years in prison for a series of armed robberies committed in Los Angeles during college breaks. And less than a year after the Dunster House deaths, a second suicide/homicide occurred in California between two Harvard graduates of the class of '93, when Chinua Sanyika, an African-American first-year Stanford medical student, murdered his college sweetheart and former classmate, Anthea Williams, a native South African, and then killed himself. Friends recalled the two as having been "inseparable"; a suicide note was left suggesting that the killings were prompted by a love triangle.

Since 1992, federal law has required all colleges to make public their annual crime statistics—a law proposed by Security on Campus, a national organization founded by a couple after their daughter was murdered at Lehigh University in Pennsylvania in 1986. The latest available statistics, from 1995, on crimes committed on Harvard campus include 5 forcible sex offenses; 28 aggravated assaults; 7 robberies; 86 burglaries; 13 car thefts; 16 drug busts; and 2 arrests for illegal weapons. The year before included 5 forcible sex offenses; 45 aggravated assaults; 6 robberies; 99 burglaries; 17 car thefts; 15 drug busts; and 11 arrests for illegal weapons.

An article on crime at Harvard in *Swing* magazine stated that "a recurring theme . . . was that Harvard wanted the stories kept quiet," and quoted Dean Jewett as saying, "We generally feel that this is a private matter between the student and the institution." *Swing* notes that Harvard shifts "into action only once they face the prospect of offending philanthropic alumni. That's meant a policy of heel-dragging and downplaying until events hit the news."

C rime, obviously, does not enhance a university's reputation. Following a campus slaying at Johns Hopkins last April, sixteen students withdrew initial acceptances to the school. When three students from Morehouse College in Atlanta were murdered in 1994, Morehouse suffered a precipitous decline in applicants the following year, which the college tried to combat by holding nationwide meetings in a dozen cities. "Higher education is a reputational product," Morton Owen Schapiro, a dean at the University of Southern California who specializes in studying institutions of higher learning, told the *New York Times*.

There is no other school in the country whose reputation is

greater—and more carefully cultivated—than Harvard's. Reputation and money form a kind of dialectic: the richer Harvard gets, the more it has the resources to attract top faculty and students who enhance its reputation; the higher its reputation, the easier it is to fund-raise. The Dunster House deaths occurred in the midst of a five-year $2.1 billion fund-raising drive—with a stated goal of a million dollars a day—a sum unprecedented in academia, but perhaps possible for Harvard. The year of the deaths Harvard had ranked first in contributions among universities and seventh nationally in contributions received by all organizations.

Although its endowment of nearly $9 billion is the largest of any university in the country, Harvard's need for money is enormous. Its annual operating costs of $1.4 billion are about the same as the entire budget of the Ethiopian government. As an administrator explains, "There are a lot more claims on Harvard's money than on any other college. Teaching undergraduates is a very small part of what Harvard does. A school like Princeton or the University of Texas may actually have more money to spend on their students than we do."

Harvard College is a fraction of Harvard University, which supports ten graduate schools, many museums, and the largest private library in the country. While some of the university's graduate schools, such as the business and law schools, produce alumni who often become wealthy and make large contributions, those gifts are often restricted to their schools. The graduates of the divinity or education schools, on the other hand, rarely become big donors, and those schools tend to drain money from the university at large.

Moreover, the administrator says, "there isn't another college in the country that tries to maintain this number of national museum-quality treasures. Harvard has the Trojan Horse syndrome—they couldn't refuse incredible gifts that ended up costing them enormous amounts of money." For example, Harvard has a three-thousand piece collection of glass flowers—the only of its kind in the world; it was a donation, of course, but one that requires a great deal of museum space and also dusting.

Harvard also has "over three thousand course offerings" and "endowed chairs in obscure subjects where the chair didn't begin to cover the cost of the subject." There is a professor and an associate professor of Assyriology, for example—among the world's leading experts on Assyrian and Old Babylonian language and culture. Eighteen courses are offered in Akkadian, including Elementary Akkadian, Intermediate Akkadian, Akkadian Divination Texts, Old Akkadian and Eblaite, and Peripheral Akkadian. There are also a half dozen courses in Sumerian and a smattering in Hittite as well.

In other schools, when a course lacks students it is eliminated, but part of the ideology of academia at Harvard is that course offerings are not determined by the marketplace. "If there are no students interested in a subject, perhaps it is because they are ignorant," a professor tells me. "And they may be interested next year, or next decade. We're trying to keep the candle in the darkness flickering. The university isn't just a place to service students; it has a mission of scholarship and the pursuit of knowledge."

That mission requires, among other things, a commitment to maintaining the Harvard University Library, whose nearly one hundred libraries constitute the world's largest university library and the largest library in America after the Library of Congress, "the scale and scope of which is," a Harvard administrator says, "a glory and a curse." The library's twelve million volumes—including rare books such as a First Folio of Shakespeare and a Gutenberg Bible—require "an incredible amount of upkeep. You can't suddenly stop collecting all the new books on ancient Greek, for example, or the old collection gets out of date."

More recent expenses at Harvard she explains as being tied to "the managerial revolution—the huge number of new managers they've brought in. It's an iron law of bureaucracy that it grows," she says. "There's no downsizing because the managers can't downsize the faculty because they're tenured and they won't downsize themselves."

The 1994 hiring of James H. Rowe III, '73, to handle public affairs at a salary of more than $200,000 a year, with an expense account of tens of thousands of dollars, was part of this managerial revolution. Traditionally, administrators had been drawn from the ranks of academics. They all held Ph.D.s—not because the job required a knowledge of Reformation history, but out of a general belief that scholars would be more likely to share the values of an academic institution. But in recent years, the administrator explained to me, managers like Rowe "with backgrounds in law or lobbying have been brought in to manage things that have nothing to do with students or faculty or culture. There is a disassociation between the managers and what should be the business of a university."

Part of the ideology of the new managers—a technique imported from the world outside the academy—is a belief in the importance of spin control. An administrator explains: "It used to be they were too proud to try to control the press. Harvard's alumni magazine used to be very critical of the administration. There was not another college magazine in the country like that. But that's all changed." The news office used to be run by one laid-back woman for whom handling the press seemed mainly to involve telling reporters, "Professor Jones is delighted to have won the Nobel Prize. He is available for interviews." But, as an administrator explains, "Rowe—a former Washington lawyer and NBC lobbyist—believes in a greater degree of spin control than any previous person in that position."

After the Dunster House deaths, the news office could have adopted the line that every institution has troubled students and Harvard is, alas, no exception. Instead it chose to propagate the idea that the student didn't appear to have any troubles and the tragedy had, therefore, no explanation. And to ensure that no contradictory information emerged, the news office had to make sure no one talked—as it were—out of school.

Harvey Silverglate, a Boston trial lawyer and the coauthor of a book on the state of liberty on American college campuses who has been an affiliate of Dunster House for the past fifteen years, believes, "The fact that the university has sent the word out not to talk to anyone [about the Dunster House deaths] is precisely part of the problem. The outrage is that they're more interested in preserving the reputation of the university when their real interest should be in getting people to talk about it as much as possible to figure out what went wrong."

As for Jewett's comment to me about the necessity to centralize information: "Fifteen years ago he would not have said that—he would have been embarrassed." But Harvey Silverglate has watched how "during that time the whole university has gradually become a portfolio of securities and real estate to which is incidentally attached an educational institution. Faculty have drawn back in their historic role of setting policy and running the institution. The administrators have taken over Harvard. Everything is calculated to minimize negative publicity and is managed by lawyers, whose main concern is 'no trouble on my watch.' Harvard has eleven full-time house lawyers. The office of chief counsel is right next to Rudenstine's. Consequently various humane and educational values—such as self-criticism and truth-telling—are subordinated to protecting the university's reputation."

MIT, on the other hand, he says, does not have an office of general counsel. They rely on outside counsel when necessary. The result, he feels, is that advice from MIT lawyers is much more narrowly directed toward specific legal problems—as legal advice should be. "If they took the office of the general counsel and used it for student services they'd be much better off," he says.

A stately red brick Georgian building, with strings of dark double rooms, a dark wood-paneled library, sunken dining room, and shadowed courtyard, Dunster House somehow lends itself to the word "haunted." One of the farthest houses from Harvard yard, the center of campus, Dunster is known to attract serious students—the kind who rarely emerge from their rooms. As an undergraduate, I recall telling myself that my problems were mine, but in my mind it was *the place* that was depressive, and my senior year I moved to another house and was glad to be gone.

Modeled after the college system of Oxford and Cambridge, Harvard's houses were built in the first part of the century when the dormitories in Harvard Yard became full. Freshmen are all housed in the Yard, after which they choose a house. Each of the houses acquired a distinctive character. Eliot House had had a long tradition as being the preppy house, Adams House the artsy one, Kirkland House the one for jocks, and so forth (although these characters are being dispelled, for in an effort to combat the stereotypes the administration decided to randomize housing—a policy that went into effect the year after the murder).

Two students affiliated with Dunster House had committed suicide two days apart the month before the murder/suicide—a fact no one knew what to make of. Ashwini Sukthankar describes Dunster House as "very intense. A lot of depressed people, very hard-working, quiet, angst-ridden, extremely incestuous—people at Dunster mainly hang out with each other—a lot of Asian students, some musical ones." Karen Hullenbaugh, the assistant to the master, described Dunster House to the press as "the weirdest house on campus: artistic, eclectic, off the beaten path. A lot of students around campus are saying they're not surprised it happened at Dunster House, if any house."

Although the house ambiance existed long before I lived there, Leslie Dunton-Downer tells me that in recent years "students have seized that darkness and tried to make it their own: there's a late-late-night café, a house opera, and a rites-of-spring goat roast, where the goat is eaten with paleolithic implements." She herself is fascinated by "the mythology of darkness that makes people believe it had to happen in Dunster House," and the way in which this case "collaborates in that mythology. What's frightening from a cultural standpoint is that mythologies are true or become true or people make them true because they believe them—because the rumor is codetermining," as in a house with a culture of suicide.

The day before commencement, a warm cloudy day, nine days after the murder, I go to Dunster House to request an interview with the master, Karel Liem. None of the people I knew at Dunster are still there, but the house looks just the same. The doors of all the entryways are flung open; students and their families are in the process of moving out, a bereft and weary gaiety on their faces. The year is over, summer here.

I go to the house office, where the assistant to the master, Carol Finn, receives visitors and handles house business. I explain that I am writing an article and I would like to interview Master Liem. She glares at me—a stout, short, white-haired woman who has been working there a long time. She tells me she will relay the message to the master.

I notice the house telephone directory lying on the coffee table and ask to look at it to get the telephone numbers of tutors in the house I want to contact.

"No, you may not! We do not want you contacting anyone! We need to protect our students and staff from reporters!" Her voice has risen to a pitch. I decide to leave.

On the way out, I notice the same telephone directory by the house phone at the entrance to the house. I had forgotten it is kept there so that visitors can call students in their rooms and ask them to come out and meet them. A guard lounging in the sun smiles at me. I open it and copy some numbers into my notebook. I can get the numbers from Harvard information, of course, simply by calling the operator, but I take particular pleasure in getting it from the book Carol Finn had been so protective of.

A few days later I receive a phone call from James H. Rowe III, vice-president for government, community, and public affairs. He says that he wants to meet with me—he works with all the press. He helped Jane Mayer with a *New Yorker* piece on Gina Grant, he says, and asks if I know Jane. I say no. I am surprised though—I had read the piece, and I thought I recalled that it had no quotes from anyone at Harvard, stating that Harvard considered all questions relating to admissions confidential.

I prepare for the meeting, drawing up a list of questions and facts I want to verify, such as which courses Sinedu had gotten the medical excuses for and whether those excuses were psychological or physiological ones. On the appointed day, I go to Massachusetts Hall, an exquisite eighteenth-century house, the oldest surviving Harvard building. I sit waiting in the front room, decorated like a drawing room with flowers and polished antiques—the kind of room that makes one wish to be wearing a dress. Half an hour later, I am ushered into a small room where Jim Rowe and Joe Wrinn, who works under him in the news office, are waiting—middle-aged white men in suits. I take out my notebook.

Jim Rowe begins to speak. He has received a number of calls about me, he says. People at Harvard are extremely concerned that I might *misuse* my insider status in order to find out confidential information about the university. He has received a call from Master Liem complaining that I infiltrated myself into Dunster House and attempted to obtain confidential information.

I lose my breath a little. "I went to the house office and asked for an interview," I say, trying to rethink the brief conversation. "I asked to look at the house phone directory."

Rowe tells me that Master Liem didn't specify the exact nature of the information, but he is certain it is a good deal more confidential than a telephone directory. His voice brims with sarcasm. He asks if I always tell people I am a reporter before I talk to them.

"Of course. How else would I request an interview?"

Rowe asks who else I have spoken to, and I tell him a few tutors. He asks which tutors and then, holding up his hand, says that no, I'm not required to reveal my sources.

"No, I will, I don't mind," I say quickly. Suddenly determined to make a show of a clean hand, I give him the names of the three tutors I have spoken to. He jots them down and says he will verify I told them all I was a reporter and get back to me. After all, he adds, you have many connections to Harvard—you are wearing many hats. People might mistake you for a tutor or a student and confide in you.

Joe Wrinn isn't saying much; I wonder what his function is. I wonder if this was how students felt being called in to the Ad Board—the board dealing with disciplinary infractions. I had been a rule-abiding student, though, and never crossed any administrators. I recall the big informational meeting shortly after the deaths when I had first had a sense that the assignment would change my relationship to Harvard—and I could see now that it had.

It had been strange for me, working on this story, to realize that I was writing about a girl whose experience at Harvard had not been analogous to my own. I loved Harvard and felt cosseted and nurtured by it. I loved doing my homework in the stacks of Widener Library, across from Memorial Church and Emerson Hall, whose red brick is inscribed: "What Is Man That Thou Art Mindful of Him?"—a question whose answer seemed in many ways to lie in the volumes of Widener. I loved having lunch with my father at the Faculty Club at the start of each term, eating Indian pudding and discussing what courses I should take—and realizing that by the next such occasion I would know something about each of the subjects we chose. I loved a house that Harvard owns on a small island off the coast of Maine—a gift from some Victorian alumni—that faculty can use in the summer. You get off the boat and a sign with an arrow says "Harvard," and points to a path through the woods. In the cupboard is blue Wedgwood china with little pictures of old Harvard buildings on it. The house was a gift to Harvard by the same family that endowed a fellowship I received when I graduated, the Briggs-Copeland Literary Traveling Fellowship, which sent me to Ireland, where I wrote poetry and learned to ride horseback.

But investigative journalism involves, at some fundamental level, going places where you are not wanted—where people react with fear and dismay—and have reason to. And when those places are your places, you know you will never be able to go back in the same way again. Leaving Massachusetts Hall that day, I knew, with a sense of loss, I would never feel quite the same about the school again.

A few days later Jim Rowe calls me at home and tells me I can forget the meeting. He has checked with the tutors whose names I had given him and they have confirmed that I introduced myself as a reporter. He also talked with Carol Finn and found out that what I had asked for was the phone directory after all, and he agrees with me that it is not a confidential document. As a result, he says, he has taken no action against me. I ask what kind of action he could take, and he says that he could call *The New Yorker* and complain. I am struck, once again, by the aggression of his tone—how unacademic a style it is. The old breed of administrators played power games, too, of course, but they kept them hidden beneath their shirt sleeves. I express surprise that Harvard has that much control over the press and he assures me that it does.

Soon afterward, several of the tutors I had spoken to call me back and ask me to make their interviews anonymous because Karel Liem had held a meeting in which he told them not to talk to the press, and they were afraid they would be fired if he found out—as he had fired tutors in the past for talking to *The Crimson* about previous problems in the house. One tutor tells me tearfully that she had lied to Master Liem and said that she hadn't spoken to anyone and she doesn't want me to use her interview at all now—even anonymously. A rule of journalism is that statements made knowingly on the record cannot be retracted—or your story would be continually disappearing as all your sources had second thoughts. But I decide to take it as my punishment for having disclosed the tutor's name and write the phrase that journalists hate, "Not for Quotation," in my notebook at the top of her interview.

P aranoia at Dunster House was not a new thing. By the time of the murder/suicide, Karel Liem was running scared. The Henry Bryant Bigelow Professor of Ichtyology and curator of the 1.2 million specimens of fish at the Museum of Comparative Zoology—the largest collection of fishes from the Atlantic Ocean— Liem was a man much more adept at classifying dead sea-life than dealing with human problems. The murder/suicide was the climax of a tenure at Dunster House that, as one tutor put it, "could only be described as disastrous," during which the university had considered the unprecedented move of firing the house master.

In the spring leading up to the murder/suicide, Liem had been taxed by two suicides and a number of attempts. In April, Katherine Louise Tucker—who had graduated the previous year, but who had stayed around the house to continue her extracurricular activities— had opened her veins in a bathtub in a local hotel room. She had suffered from a long-term depression and been counseled extensively at Dunster House and at the University Health Services.

Two days later sophomore Ansgar Hansen had thrown himself under a Cambridge subway train. The fact that Ansgar lived off campus was used to downplay his relationship to the house, but John Sindall, the former Dunster House assistant to the senior tutor, Suzi Naiburg, recalls that in the last months of his life Ansgar had been counseled extensively by Suzi Naiburg. In the week preceding his death Ansgar had spent several hours with her daily; they were supposed to meet the day he committed suicide. "I felt she wasn't qualified to counsel him," Sindall says. "If he had a psychological problem, he should have been counseled by a psychiatrist."

After Ansgar's death, Sindall was shocked to hear Naiburg publicly denying she had counseled Ansgar at all. (Calls from me to Naiburg were returned to the news office.) Sindall was given instructions not to discuss Ansgar's death with anyone and, in response to inquiries, to read a statement put out by the news office. Ansgar's parents, he recalls, were "quickly quieted from the top." Sindall feels "there should have been an investigation after Ansgar's death," and "that that lack of investigation resulted in more deaths." Then, after Sinedu and Trang's deaths, he says, "I watched them once again covering their tracks." Of all the deaths, the murder/suicide had the most potential to be damaging and therefore the most to cover up.

From the outset Liem seemed terrified that the deaths would be pinned on him and his administration. Shortly after the murder/suicide, he held a televised press conference in which he said that the whole event had been very hard on *him*. People don't understand, he said, as a house master, one gets quite attached to the students.

What was hard on him, of course, was his own sense of responsibilty and the excessive efforts to deny it he felt compelled to make. "I had no inkling there was a problem," he told *Boston* magazine. "If anyone should have known, I should have known. I'm the master of the house. I'm very accessible. I was their academic advisor. . . . You'd think I would have detected something. But I never did. . . . That she [Sinedu] could keep [her problems] to herself without any indication to others, I find it remarkable."

According to the *Dunster House Book*, the house master is "responsible for the overall management and well-being of the House Community." As the head of a house of over three hundred students, the master cannot really be expected to know every student, each of whom is supposed to be kept closer track of by an assigned academic adviser—ordinarily tutors who live in the house. However, as luck would have it, Liem was Trang and Sinedu's academic adviser, so his general responsibility as house master was combined in this case with a specific responsibility.

Liem told the *New York Times* that he and Suzi Naiburg, the senior tutor, knew the roommates were splitting up, but neither had come to them with reports of rancor. He said that he knew of no special problems Sinedu had been having and, in fact, had met with Sinedu three days before her death. The final entry in the *Dunster House Book*, "A Few Last Helpful Hints," states: "If a student looks unwell or particularly unhappy and says he/she is 'fine' when this is obviously not the case, asking the question a second time (e.g. saying 'Are you sure?') often has the effect of letting the student know that you actually care."

At the end of his meeting with Sinedu, Liem told the press, he asked his standard question: was anything making her unhappy? Quickly, he says, Sinedu told him no, gave him a big smile, and left. But as a tutor commented, "Liem is not the kind of person anyone would confide in. He likes to think of himself as a hearty open person, yet it's all fake. He is very self-deluding and out of touch. He likes to pretend everything is fine in the house when actually things are very bad. He just doesn't want to know."

Liem also told Elie Kaunfer, working for the *New York Times*, that Sinedu never went to Mental Health Service at Harvard. He planned to make no administrative changes in Dunster House, he said, because the tutorial staff was "excellent." He described the deaths as "a real tragedy and a real mystery," and concluded, "We will probably never know what the underlying factor is."

The police found the letter to the stranger in Sinedu's file at Dunster House. It had been forwarded there from the freshman dean's office, where it had been inspected by a dean and then passed on to Liem. As her adviser, Liem was responsible for familiarity with the contents of her file. A law enforcement official recalls Liem telling the police that he had never mentioned the letter to Sinedu directly, but that he and Suzi Naiburg had used the letter as a "heads-up" on how to deal with her.

As senior tutor, Suzi Naiburg was "responsible for academic progress and personal well-being of individual students in the house." She was out of town at the time of the murder; although the term was not yet over, she had left for vacation in New Mexico a few days previously. She had counseled Trang on several occasions that spring about her rooming troubles.

John Sindall recalls that, starting in February, Sinedu came into the house office several times to talk to Carol Finn, who was in charge of housing. After Ansgar Hansen's death, Sindall had become more sensitive to depression, and he was struck by Sinedu's blank affect. She took no notice of the aquarium he had in his office, which students were often fascinated by. Ordinarily, he knew how to make students laugh—he wore funny ties and would joke with them, but Sinedu would respond momentarily, smiling perfunctorily, her face immediately reverting to its blank state. "When I left Vietnam," Sindall, a former Vietnam vet, says, "I resolved to myself that I would never hold a gun again and I would never see another dead teenager. By the time that year was out, I had seen four."

After my article appeared in *The New Yorker,* on the first anniversary of the deaths, the news office released a statement in response to press inquiries which did not address any specifics of my story but stated, "Based on what we knew then, we remain confident that appropriate steps were taken." But a reporter from *The Crimson* called and told me that Master Liem had given them an interview responding to my article in which he stated that he had never seen the letter to the stranger in Sinedu's file, he knew nothing about the rooming changes, and all my information had been found out in an illicit manner, by trespassing in the house and sneaking past the security guard in search of confidential information.

I abstained from comment (which would create a "controversy," and therefore constitute a story) and sent Master Liem an angry fax, after which he telephoned me. I reminded him what had happened during my only visit to Dunster House, a year previously, and he swiftly began to backtrack.

"Carol did not tell me the nature of the confidential document— I had thought perhaps it was the girls' files, or some such thing," he said. "But the telephone directory—ah yes—no, no, that is not a problem."

He also agreed that it hadn't been improper for me to go to the house office to request an interview. "If it was up to us, we would have been very open about the whole thing, of course," he said, "but the news office didn't want us talking to the press." Immediately after the murder a guard was posted outside the house who was supposed to question anyone who didn't look like a student or tutor or faculty member—a policy Master Liem explained that had never worked. The reporter from *People* magazine, he said, had actually walked past the guard and into the living room of the master's private residence because the reporter was wearing blue jeans, so the guard mistook him for a graduate student. By the time of my visit they had stopped the policy altogether because too many people were coming in and out for commencement, and the rest of the press had already left campus anyway. But Liem was standing by the other things he had told *The Crimson,* he said.

"I know nothing of the letter you referred to in Sinedu's file or any request for a change of roommates," he said.

A moment of silence occurred and then I took a breath and said: "Didn't you tell the police you had read Sinedu's letter to the stranger, and you had never discussed it with Sinedu, but you used it as a 'heads-up' in dealing with her?"

I could hardly believe I was calling a professor on a bald-faced lie. It felt both rude and excessively intimate, somehow—I didn't know him well enough to address him by his first name, but I was asking him not to lie to me. I could see some of the facts of the deaths would make him uncomfortable, and if he could do things over again, he should, but I hadn't been of the opinion that what I knew of his role was that damning. A murder/suicide is inevitably the culmination of a long intricate chain of events: by definition, if any of the links had been different the chain might have been broken, but that doesn't mean that any specific individual can ultimately be held responsible for the killings besides the killer. Letters that include phrases like "if I live" should not be simply filed away, but Sinedu was already in counseling at the time—a much more integral link in the chain. But Liem's obfuscation seemed to put things in a more ominous light and call his credibility generally into account.

He began to speak rapidly. "No, no, I don't recall Sinedu's letter," he said. "There was another letter from the freshman dean's office, describing Sinedu as a troubled student—that was the heads-up I was referring to. Perhaps I misspoke to the police—I was under a great deal of stress at the time. I have a heart condition." He also said that he hadn't meant that Trang hadn't requested a rooming change. "I only said that I never saw the rooming change *form* on my desk," he said.

I asked him to call *The Crimson* and correct some misapprehensions they might have. He assured me that he would and we hung up.

The reporter called me back later that night and said that Liem hadn't changed his story. I called Liem again and he told me that he had, but in case they had misunderstood, he would call again—which he did, and after which *The Crimson* called again and said the story remained intact and that if Liem had said he had changed his story he was telling me something different than he was telling them.

Yet another round of phone calls were exchanged and in the morning the story appeared, more or less just as it had been, with the headline: "Dunster Officials Criticize Reporter." The confidential document I had sought had been changed from the telephone directory to "a list of tutors," and although the story states that Carol Finn refused to give it to me, and that therefore my attempt at gathering information was "somewhat unsuccessful," nevertheless the Dunster House administration felt my "very presence in the House" constituted a "violation." There was even a quote from the superintendent, saying that he thought he recalled me having come to the house a year ago and telling him I was a tutor, and that otherwise I never would have been let in.

There was an early morning message on my machine from Liem as well: "This is Karel Liem calling. I read the *Crimson* article. . . . I want you to know I certainly never said any of those things . . . but I guess they did not want to listen to me."

I listened to the message several times, amazed at the compulsion that would make someone publicly proclaim falsehoods and then offer, unbidden, a taped retraction to the subject of their slander—the person least likely to believe them, who could only respond with irritation and confusion.

L iem and Naiburg were not the only people whose responsibilities included Sinedu and Trang's welfare; there was also an "entryway tutor" in the house—a resident tutor responsible for the students living in their domain—and a premedical adviser—a medical student who provided advice and guidance. That year there were sixteen tutors living in Dunster House—primarily graduate students who, in exchange for free room and board, were supposed to provide the personal contact and academic advice a student may miss in a big school. The *Dunster House Book* states: "For students, the tutor can be a teacher, a role model, a policeman, a friend."

The 1993 "Dunster House Tutor Guide" distributed to all the tutors instructs them that "on the subject of files, it is a good idea to look at the files of your advisees to familiarize yourself with their recent history—Harvard application essays make interesting reading and can be quite revealing." Entryway tutors are instructed to "get to know all the students in your entryway . . . well enough so that you can inquire after their well-being if they look unwell as they attempt to scuttle by you late at night."

The book has an odd tone for a counseling handbook (the instruction to look at students' files because they make for "interesting reading"; students "scuttling" as if they are cockroaches). The guide concludes with a final injunction to "never ever play a practical joke on Karel."

In the wake of the deaths many students expressed anger that, as Ashwini Sukthankar put it, "the tutor system let Sinedu slip through the cracks." William James said that "the thinkers in their youth are almost always very lonely creatures," but that "the University most worthy of admiration is that one in which your lonely thinker can feel himself least lonely . . . and most richly fed." It's a tricky mixture: supporting solitude—and a question around which colleges tend to define themselves.

Harvard follows the watchmaker model of God: students are admitted to the kingdom, with all its marvels, and allowed to make of it what they will. A Gregory McDonald novel from the sixties opens with a Harvard student watching his roommate slit his wrists, and reading a book. He finishes the chapter, checks that his roommate is dead, and then calls the police. He explains to the authorities that he regrets that his roommate is dead, but he hadn't wanted to interfere with his roommate's plans—he thought his roommate should be free to do as he chose. The administration can't decide whether his attitude constitutes any infraction for which the student should be punished—or whether it is, in some way, in the Harvard tradition.

"Harvard is what it is," a tutor told me. "Students should know what they're choosing when they come here." Another tutor said, "I see students all the time who are desperately unhappy—who would have been much better off at a smaller school, but they got into Harvard. It's as if the weight of that acceptance letter left them no options—you get into Harvard, you have to come." Leslie Dunton-Downer says simply, "Students who want a lot of hand-holding should have gone somewhere else. There are real limits to what the tutors can do."

Diep Nguyen, a friend of Trang's, says that there is "very little contact between tutors and students. They usually meet once or twice a year." Another student commented, "You'd think, after all the previous suicides in Dunster House, someone would have sent the tutors a memo, saying 'Hello, wake-up call,'" but then again, his own tutor "couldn't pick me out of a police lineup."

Tutors are busy law or medical or doctoral students whose primary commitment is to their own work. And even when tutors do make time for them, students—particularly Harvard students—often feel a conflict about confiding in the people who control their files and are supposed to be writing their recommendations. Moreover, tutors are not chosen because they're interested in counseling: they're chosen on the basis of their academic qualifications.

David Lombard, a busy M.D./Ph.D. candidate at Harvard Medical School, happened to live in Trang and Sinedu's entryway and so he was their entryway tutor, as well as their premedical adviser. According to their friends, neither girl was close to him. He was one of two male resident premedical tutors and eight male nonresident premedical tutors. There were no female premedical tutors—a ratio which was a source of student protest at the time of Lombard's hiring because there were a large number of female premedical students at Dunster, some of whom preferred to work with a woman. Of the whole resident tutorial staff in Dunster House that year, only three of the sixteen tutors were female.

Lombard told police interviewers that both Trang and Sinedu had taken the MCATs that spring and Sinedu had sent out a few medical school applications. He said that he had last seen the roommates around April 26, that relations between them were "cordial" at that time, and that he had noticed no problems.

For a number of years preceding the murder, Dunster had been embroiled in a series of staffing scandals—the details of which are good examples of the kind of web Master Liem tends to entangle himself within. In 1993, Liem allowed Vince Li, a premedical tutor with whom he had a strong alliance, to prevail on him to hire Li's brother, girlfriend, and a childhood friend to be tutors in the house, angering the other tutors and students and leading to complaints of nepotism. The conflict was depicted in a series of articles in *The Crimson*, in which Liem insisted that the new tutors had been hired on their own merits and Vince Li hadn't been involved in the decision at all. Liem was caught in a number of embarrassing inconsistencies when tutors recalled that Li had actually been present at one of his brother's interviews with a house committee. At another point Liem claimed he had had student support for the candidates, when students had actually advocated other tutors. Tutors were quoted at the time as commenting that they were "very unhappy with the atmosphere, the layering of lie after lie," and the "dishonesty brought on this house."

Liem responded to the problems by seeking to discover the tutors who had cooperated with the story in *The Crimson* and fire them. But most of the tutors had spoken anonymously, for, as one of the articles explained, "seven of the eight of the tutors contacted spoke on the condition of anonymity, saying they feared they would be fired if they spoke on the record." As one tutor told me, "Karel's response to problems was always punitive and primitive. He was the master and he had an embattled sense of defending his territory. He has a totalitarian sensibility. He always thought if he could just squelch a few more troublemakers everything would be okay. He could never allow for difference or dissent." He was referred to in the house as "Overlord Liem."

By trying to squelch problems, of course, Liem only created much more serious ones. The tutors' original complaint was hardly a devastating indictment; Liem could simply have acknowledged some impropriety—or at least the appearance of impropriety—and put the incident behind him. Instead, he pressured tutors to turn in the anonymous sources of complaint and created a divisive "witch hunt" atmosphere in the house in which tutors were split into those Liem perceived as loyal and those he regarded with suspicion.

Finally several of the tutors met with Fred Jewett, then dean of Harvard College. Jewett told them he could do nothing unless they filed a formal complaint but, according to *The Crimson*, "tutors said they did not file the complaint for fear of repercussions from the Master." The following year a large number of the staff—among them the tutors most popular with students—resigned or were "nonhired"—that is, fired, and new ones—hand-picked by Liem— came in, including David Lombard. The result of this, according to a student, was that "all the good tutors had left. The tutors who stayed were not there because they had any interest in students, but because they had sucked up to the master."

Leslie Dunton-Downer says that "in some measurable way it is possible to say the composition of tutors and different kinds of affiliates changed significantly as the result of Liem's actions. Students were not involved in the process of hiring tutors the way they should be—and had they been involved I don't think any of those tutors would have been brought in."

In a subsequent meeting with one of the fired tutors, Dean Jewett assured him that the administration understood the problems of Liem's tenure and that when his five-year contract expired at the end of the academic year, 1993–94, it would not be given the customary renewal.

When the contract did come up, however, Liem met with Jewett and insisted he wanted to retain his mastership, and Jewett backed down. A compromise was struck in which his contract was renewed for two rather than the usual five years, at which point it would come up again for reconsideration. Jewett lamely explained afterward to one of the fired tutors that "Harvard in its long history has never dismissed a sitting master and it doesn't want to start a bad precedent." Masters often hold their positions for decades—and resignation is always at their volition.

Part of the explanation may be that the administration often has difficulty finding house masters. Harvard insists on using faculty for the position, and most faculty prefer to concentrate on their scholarship, teaching, and research. A Harvard administrator explained to me that "it's hard to find house masters and senior tutors—Yale will hire from outside the faculty, but Harvard won't. It's particularly hard to find minorities—Liem played the minority card, being from Indonesia, to great effect." (Although Liem was actually Dutch, he had grown up in Indonesia, and in his *Dunster House Book* self-description he stresses the special sensitivity with which his background has endowed him—his "strong conviction to strive for cultural and racial harmony.")

A Harvard administrator says he is not surprised by Jewett's refusal to stand up to Liem. "There is an ethic of senatorial courtesy that one doesn't embarrass a faculty member. Administrators are terrified of a situation where the faculty will say: "Who are you, a Beta person, to judge an Alpha person like myself, the world-renowned, so-and-so professor of such-and-such?' Faculty members have tremendous latitude— if a faculty member goes off the deep end no one does anything. When faculty members are having trouble teaching it is unheard of for anyone to talk to them about it. You can have a professor whose lectures are incomprehensible and no one will call him on it."

The academic year 1994–95 was the first year of the renewal of Liem's contract. Thus the murder happened in the most troubled of Harvard houses, under the reign of the master least equipped to deal with it.

The identification of serious problems in students is the most important function of the staff in any student residential situation. Tutors throughout Harvard complain that they are given insufficient instruction in this area. One tutor recalls a time that "a student of mine went crazy and was taken away by the police. There had been evidence something had been going on for a long time, but I didn't know when to cross the boundary and barge into someone's room. We are given the impression that we can't do anything unless the student comes to you. If David Lombard noticed anything with Sinedu, I doubt he would have known what to do."

Dr. Elizabeth Reid, the director of consultation and liaison in the Mental Health Service at the University Health Services (UHS), says that she herself used to conduct seminars, so that "the house staff was all exposed to ongoing training, but the program was cut." She thinks that "for all kinds of troubles it would be helpful if the older people living around were knowledgeable enough and present enough to recognize signs of distress and either know what to do or know how to find out what to do. I would hope the follow-up of this incident would be a great deal more of that, and they should pay for it."

She describes the increasing financial pressure that psychological services at UHS have been under because mental health services "are very expensive and results are hard to quantify." In the twenty-eight years she has worked there, the caseload has increased and the staff decreased. On the advice of business school efficiency experts, students are now ordinarily seen for half an hour rather than an hour. "We have become busier and busier," she says, "we have fewer staff, we see more students, so we have to concentrate more on direct urgent care."

Dr. Graham Blaine, the former chief of UHS from 1965 to 1971, says that long-term psychotherapy and even psychoanalysis, in which patients were seen four to five times a week, had been available during his tenure. But like many mental health services all over the country, UHS was subsequently reorganized in accordance with the pressures of managed care. (And indeed the problems of a student health service in dealing with mental illness are a microcosm of the problems of managed care health facilities all over the country.) There is talk of shutting down the Mental Health Service altogether, as a cost-saving move, farming out all services to an HMO, like Pilgrim, which, as one therapist says, "shows how low on the university's priorities we are. The Orthopedics Department is costly too, but there's no talk of shutting that down."

Therapy is now available to students only on a limited basis. Those requiring long-term psychotherapy are referred outside, at which point, intimidated by cost and logistics, most students give up. When I was teaching at Harvard, students would sometimes come to me suffering from depression or other problems and I'd suggest they talk to a therapist. I would sometimes actually call UHS to set up the appointment while the student was still in my office because depression can make it difficult for the student to make the call later. I was always struck by the difficulty of scheduling an appointment—often the only time available would be a half hour at eight in the morning, a month hence, unless the students identified themselves as suicidal, in which case they could go to the walk-in clinic and wait several hours for emergency service. When I would talk to the students again, after they had been seen, they'd often complain that the doctor hadn't had time to really talk to them.

Lloyd Marcom, the Dunster House senior who first encountered Thao bleeding in the courtyard after the murder, says: "You get referred to outside counseling, which costs money a lot of students don't have. Or you get pressured to take time off. I don't know why they don't put more into UHS—maybe they don't think Harvard students have serious problems."

A former UHS therapist confirms, "There was an assumption that our job was basically to treat the worried well—that whatever students' problems were, they were still Harvard students, which I found untrue. The particular form of their pathology may include a high-functioning persona, but that doesn't mean it's any less serious."

The forces that lead a young person to unusual achievements are, of course, not the same forces that constitute psychological well-being. The Harvard admissions committee selects highly individualized types, many of whom were child prodigies, rose from the ghetto, are Iranian royalty, or in some other way have led unusual lives, so that as a result they are outstanding scholars, cellists, mathematicians, poets, opera singers, or goalkeepers. The steadily rising applicant pool means that the successful applicants are increasingly "special."

Dean of Students Archie Epps III tells me about a study that shows that twenty years ago most Harvard students ranked "enjoyment of life" as one of their highest priorities on a questionnaire about their goals at college and "mastery of subject" as far down on the list; today those priorities are reversed. Yet high achievement often leads to—or is a product of—isolation. Achievement can stem from insecurity—a need to prove oneself better than everyone else, or from depression—a need to make oneself feel better—as much as it can from talent or desire to contribute to the world.

Suicide statistics are tricky; many universities—including Harvard—don't disclose them and the small numbers make interpretation unreliable. Studies vary, but a number place the national average for suicides on college campuses as 6–7 out of every 100,000.[2] Thus, with an undergraduate enrollment of 6,000, Harvard should expect to have one suicide every two and a half years. Sinedu's suicide was the third among undergraduates alone at Harvard that year—the fourth if one includes Katherine Tucker—and according to Dr. Catlin, one of about twenty attempts. It was an unusually unlucky year, from which one cannot draw meaningful statistical conclusions, but suicide can certainly be said to be a serious problem at Harvard, as it is everywhere—and one that should be a cause for reflection.

Dominic Armijo, Katherine Tucker, and Ansgar Hansen—the three students who committed suicide before Sinedu that year—were all in treatment at UHS at the time of their deaths. Dominic Armijo, a senior in Kirkland House, who hanged himself that January, had actually spent the night at UHS, but his doctors decided to release him to take exams, whereupon he killed himself. At a meeting with grieving students at Kirkland House, Dr. Catlin told them not to reproach themselves because, after all, they at UHS hadn't realized the severity of Dominic's problems—a rationale students didn't find particularly comforting.

Dr. Catlin has several explanations as to why Sinedu's therapy was so inadequate. In part, he says, her therapist, Dr. Powell, didn't know Sinedu well because he saw her only on a limited basis. Also the health service is oriented toward and trained in dealing with ordinary neurotic problems of adjustment, not psychoses. "The health service is primarily set up to deal with problems of adjustment, which is what most students who come in here are suffering from," Dr. Catlin says. "From my understanding, Sinedu was being seen here because she wanted help learning how to relate to people—how to be a better student at Harvard. She was a foreign student and she was lonely. She had a big cultural adjustment to make." He says that it is his recollection that she had not been given any type of medication.

Foreign students are often at risk for undertreatment because mental disorders may be misinterpreted as assimilation problems, clinical depression as loneliness, and character pathology as traits of a foreign culture. Dr. Tedla Wolde Giorgis is director of the Multicultural Services Division, Commission on Mental Health Service, in Washington, D.C., and the author of a book on Ethiopians and depression. He stresses that, in a time in which schools have increasingly large foreign student populations, their mental health services need to have counselors who are "not just cross-culturally sensitive, but cross-culturally competent."

"Unless we understand each other's background, we're not going to be able to help," he says. Foreign students are often reluctant to go to health services, so that by the time they do "they're usually very desperate." Yet they are much less likely to communicate their state of mind—they often have trouble speaking of personal problems, and describe them instead as physical complaints.

Dr. Giorgis says that "one sees a lot more depression with a multi-ethnic population, much more so than in white Americans or African-Americans. Depression is the most prominent response that the immigrant state of dislocation brings about." The standard textbook on manic depression—Goodwin and Jamison's *Manic-Depressive Illness*—states that "the incidence of affective [mood] disorders in those who immigrated to the United States was almost twice as great as among natives."

There is some evidence that different ethnic groups are prone to different mental illnesses (the most extensive studies have concerned affective disorders in Ashkenazic Jews). Dr. Giorgis says that different ethnic groups respond differently to medication as well, which he takes into account when treating patients. For example, he says,

"Asians are more sensitive to benzodiazepines and show greater side effects with anti-depressants and Ethiopians respond best to neuleptics when given in combination with anti-depressants." He speculates on whether the change from the tropical climate of Ethiopia to the States could trigger Seasonal Affective Disorder (depression linked to sunlight deprivation).

Dr. Giorgis believes that working with a multicultural population requires a much more aggressive outreach. "When a patient drops out of treatment at our clinic, we'll call to see how they're doing—we'll even stop by their house. If they say they're fine when we get there, we'll leave. But a lot of times they don't say they're fine."

A former admissions officer at Harvard tells me that the admissions committee makes an effort not to admit students with serious mental problems—a policy they feel reluctant to broadcast for fear of accusations of discrimination. (Thus the official explanation for the retraction of Gina Grant's admission was not that she was a murderer, but only that she had lied on her application.)

"We try and discern the degree of their problems," the former admissions officer tells me. "Sometimes we send their applications over to Dr. Catlin to look at. If their problems were not that serious, we would sometimes refer to them as 'a teacup,' meaning they seemed psychologically fragile, but if they had a great many other strengths—say were a prodigy or something—we might admit them anyway. But others we sometimes called 'kitchen cabinets'—meaning there was a much larger potential for things breaking—and those we wouldn't admit under any circumstances."

amian M. Schloming, class of '98, is an example of a student who proved to be a kitchen cabinet. The story he tells of his experience, and the stories of Charles Truesdell, '99, and Seth Mnookin, class of '94, reveal something of Harvard's incompetence at dealing with students suffering from psychiatric disorders. Damian's problems began immediately after he arrived at Harvard, when, as a practical joke, the guys who lived across the hall from him sent obscene E-mail to a number of freshman women in Damian's name. Then they broke into his room and put up pornographic images of women. Damian called the police, who, instead of filing a report, handed the matter over to the freshman dean's office (police reports contribute to the campus statistics on crime, which schools prefer to keep as low as possible).

The assistant dean of freshmen, Christina Griffith, told Damian that as a woman she was very offended by the obscenity. She seemed very interested in punishing the perpetrators, but she didn't seem to Damian to take an interest in his welfare, refusing to even discuss getting him a new room. Meanwhile, with the guys across the hall facing disciplinary action, tensions escalated. After Damian got an E-mail message from one of the men in his entryway saying, "I want to kill you,"—a joke, perhaps, but one whose hostility seemed real—Damian's father called Christina Griffith and said, "There's a *death* threat," but she still refused to discuss getting a room change. Moving off campus was not an option financially (room and board are part of students' financial aid package).

During the conflict Damian was assigned a new adviser, John B. Fox, Jr., '59, secretary of the faculty—an important man at Harvard for several decades, whose positions have included that of dean of Harvard College and administrative dean of the Graduate School of Arts and Sciences. John Fox explained to Damian that he would not be able to move rooms because there were no extra rooms. Damian knew that Harvard—which owns more than four hundred buildings—is one of the biggest landlords in Cambridge. However, John Fox explained, housing for undergraduates is tight because the school would lose money if they used them for student housing rather than renting them out at market prices.

Unable to be in his dorm room, Damian moved back to his parents' home in Cambridge. But eventually, after enlisting the university minister, Reverend Gomes, along with a faculty member of the business school to plead for him, Damian won and was given a new room. But the battle he had had to fight struck Damian as absurd, and he wrote an article that he published in the *Salient*, a student magazine, entitled, "The Tyranny of the Freshman Dean's Office." After it was published, John Fox told Damian that the article had severely damaged his relationship with Harvard. Damian said he had imagined the freshman dean's office might be angry with him, but John Fox told him Harvard is a network and he had alienated the entire administration.

It was during the course of these troubles that Damian first sought counseling at the Bureau of Study Counsel—an organization that offers counseling, issue-oriented therapy groups (one of which Sinedu attended), and help with studying problems. Damian described the problems with insomnia and concentration he was experiencing. The counselor responded to them as studying problems. He did not recognize that Damian actually had a medical problem (what would later be diagnosed as a bipolar disorder) and he did not refer him to the University Health Services for evaluation.

Thus it was not until December of his sophomore year that, suffering from severe insomnia and depression, Damian first made his way to UHS. That Thanksgiving Damian's twin brother, an MIT student, had been diagnosed with bipolar disorder and had been hospitalized at McLean, a psychiatric hospital. Damian told the doctor about his brother's experience and expressed concern that he had the same disease. The doctor replied that if he was a more aggressive doctor he might give him a mood stabilizer, like lithium, but he wasn't, so he suggested Damian treat himself with Benedryl (an over-the-counter allergy remedy) and warm milk.

The next day, after another sleepless night, Damian went back to UHS. He saw another doctor, who told him he was just anxious about being bipolar because of his brother's diagnosis, and gave him a prescription for Ativan, a mild sedative. Damian's parents called the doctor and urged him to take their son's problems seriously. They could not afford to send Damian to a private doctor, which student health insurance will not pay for. A month later Damian met with the doctor again, and asked to be prescribed Depakote, with which his brother had been successfully treated. Specific symptoms are more responsive to Depakote than to lithium and Damian felt he had had those (so-called rapid-cycling manic depression, with a combination of manic and depressive symptoms).

The doctor told him he didn't know much about Depakote—a newer drug, but one that has been prescribed for a decade—and said that he felt more comfortable with lithium. So Damian spent a semester on lithium to no avail. His insomnia persisted, but the doctor continued to suggest home remedies. Finally Damian called the doctor and said, "I have stopped taking lithium, and I want a prescription for Depakote." The doctor gave it to him and Damian's symptoms rapidly abated. Through a recommendation from his brother's doctor at McLean, Damian subsequently switched to another doctor at UHS whom he likes better but who is too busy to provide the regular therapy he needs.

Throughout his ordeal, Damian felt he would have been greatly helped by the support of an understanding adviser. John Fox seemed to believe that what he had to offer as an adviser was the benefit of wisdom of his own experience as an undergraduate a quarter century before, and when Damian's problems did not conform, he became frustrated and angry with him.

The first E-mail John Fox sent Damian began: "My freshman year at Harvard was long-ago (1955–1956)! I have been a freshman adviser for over twenty-five years, however, and I am beginning to figure out how the place works. I will be happy to share any of that information which is useful to you."

In response to Damian's descriptions of his increasingly fragile state of mind, John Fox wrote back homilizing on the malaise of modern "society, with its lack of opportunities for exercise in the course of daily living." Damian had written: "I wonder if they will end up diagnosing me as 'bipolar,' like my brother. I don't very much like the label but, on the other hand, it is far better to be labeled bipolar and have no symptoms than to have the symptoms and be labeled normal." John Fox responded that Damian should "not be too eager to adopt some medical designation for yourself. . . . Most everyone feels stress at least occasionally, if not more often."

After his long struggle to get proper medication, Damian sent John Fox a bitter E-mail message:

> It is kind of funny that the best medical care in the world is provided by facilities associated with Harvard University, but when it comes to its students, Harvard provides a very different, and very special kind of care. . . . UHS Mental Health is a panacea for the (undoubtedly!) vast numbers of students who have "women's" concerns, or "ethnic" concerns or "Gay and Lesbian" concerns, but for someone who has a REAL problem, one which severely affects a student's academic life, UHS is hopelessly out of date, and, seemingly, very unwilling to provide the treatment. . . . Oh well! I suppose I

am learning strength of character and independence and, above all, individual responsibility. And I am also getting excellent clinical training as a lawyer or lobbyist, and in self-medication.

Damian continued on with general criticism of the university, to which John Fox responded:

> Damian,
> It is a pity that your diatribe about the UHS isn't amusing for then it would have at least one redeeming feature.
> Complaints about UHS, and indeed many such health organizations, are as old as the hills. I have received my medical care from the University for over forty years and am entirely satisfied. If the care provided by the UHS was as you describe it, it would have gone out of business long ago.
> Your statement that the UHS is a "panacea," for various types of concerns is, of course, offensive, as well as ignorant.
> You have said to me several times recently that you are feeling much better because of the medication you have received. Now you say that you are not being properly medicated. My conclusion is that you are not being honest with yourself or others.
> Your attacks on all things Harvard are tiresome. If you don't like it here go away.

Damian's twin brother's experience at MIT was quite different. The MIT health service had worked with McLean to provide a structure of medication and intense psychotherapy for his twin brother, without cost to the family. The MIT administration also struck the Schloming family as much more flexible. Room changes were easy to get. The Schlomings had two sons at MIT and when Damian's twin first became ill the administration allowed the youngest Schloming brother to move in with him to give him the support his illness required. The following year the two brothers were given singles near one another.

Damian's brother was able to make up the work he had missed during his hospitalization through tutoring. MIT offers free tutoring, whereas at Harvard students have to pay. Damian—who had also lost time owing to his illness—wanted tutoring but couldn't afford it. He is struck by the fact that he has not flourished academically at Harvard, whereas his brother is a star in his department at MIT, even though their mental abilities had always been similar and his brother's illness was much more severe.

An administrator at MIT tells me that they admit a great many "crazy brilliant students," and as a result they're "well set up to deal with them." In response to a number of suicides a few years back and concerns about legal action, she says, the health service underwent some changes and became much stronger.

Damian feels he would not have survived his illness had he not had a local family to support him and intervene on his behalf. "At Harvard, they're always telling you how many resources there are," he says, "and that all you have to do is seek them out. But when you're ill, you can't always fight for what you need." He feels "sympathy for Sinedu—with her parents in Ethiopia and no one to help."

The week of his final exams, May 1996, suffering from depression, Charles (Chuck) Truesdell overdosed on a bottle of Tylenol. He changed his mind, however, and aborted the attempt. He told his boyfriend, and his boyfriend thought he should go to a hospital, which he didn't want to do because he wanted to take his final exam the next day. His boyfriend prevailed, however—thus unwittingly setting in motion a long chain of events, from which Chuck has not yet extricated himself. He was taken to Mt. Auburn Hospital and then to McLean Hospital.

During his three-day stay at McLean, no Harvard official came to see him. When McLean was ready to release him, he called the dean of freshmen, Elizabeth Studley Nathans. Dean Nathans informed him that he would be given medical excuses for his final exams but that he would no longer be allowed on Harvard property. A security guard would accompany him while he vacated his room. He had previously been given permission to stay in his room through commencement, as he had a job working on the graduation issue of the *Salient*, but he was also now not allowed to work at the magazine because the building was, of course, on campus. As it happened, the summer housing that he had arranged to begin a week later was a building owned by Harvard, so he was told that plan would have to be canceled. Thus at a time when Chuck was feeling particularly vulnerable and in need of a stable environment he found himself facing homelessness. Moreover, the hospital had the sensible policy of not releasing patients until they had arranged for a place to go.

Dean Nathans referred him to Burriss Young, the associate dean of freshmen, who told him that he wished he could help him out, but Harvard lawyers had made the ruling. Chuck's freshman adviser, who lived off campus, offered to let him stay at his house for the week, but Burriss Young told him that that too would be prohibited—as his adviser was an officer of the university, the lawyers felt that if Chuck tried to hurt himself again that week the university might be held liable.

His friend Naomi Schaefer, a transfer student from Middlebury College, attempted to talk to the administration on his behalf. She encountered a typical Harvard decentralized shifting of responsibility:

several officials referred her to other officials, one of whom informed her that the decision that Chuck not be allowed on Harvard property could not be changed because it had been made by the dean of the college, Harry Lewis, who was on vacation. Naomi was struck by the contrast between the Harvard administration and that of Middlebury. "At Middlebury," she says, "you would never have a situation where everyone tells you to talk to someone in some different part of campus because the administration is small and works together and their offices are all across the hall."

The doctors at McLean assigned Chuck to the care of Dr. Catlin during the summer. Chuck quickly realized that Dr. Catlin wasn't going to be someone in whom he could confide—in part because there was no time. His first appointment with Dr. Catlin was twenty minutes; after that, Chuck was seen once every two weeks for five or ten minutes. At first he was pleased to be given so little attention because he thought that it must mean that UHS didn't think he needed much care and wasn't in bad shape. He was not put on any medication.

After his suicide attempt, Chuck had been told that, although students routinely miss exams for medical reasons and take makeups the following semester, because his medical problem had been a psychological one his return to the school was now conditional and he would have to petition the Ad Board. Dr. Catlin's recommendation, he was told, would be crucial in the decision whether to allow him to return. As he had no desire to take time off from school, Chuck was determined to impress the doctor. During each of his brief meetings with Dr. Catlin over the summer, Dr. Catlin would ask him how he was doing, and Chuck would tell him that he was fine and then Dr. Catlin would let him go.

He wasn't fine, however; as the summer wore on he became increasingly depressed. Finally, one night at the end of the summer, feeling in real need of talking to someone, he went into UHS. The therapist on call was contacted; she spoke to him on the phone and explained that she lived forty-five minutes out of town and that she wasn't going to come in just for his call, but that he should go to Cambridge City Hospital for an evaluation. Moreover, the doctor insisted he be taken to the hospital in an ambulance. He argued that he had come into UHS voluntarily and he could go to the hospital voluntarily, but she said it was university policy. He submitted, and when he arrived at the hospital, he found out that because he had arrived in an ambulance, his admission had been classified as involuntary, and that the hospital had a policy of automatically sending involuntary psychiatric admissions to McLean.

At McLean he spoke to Dr. Catlin, who told him that he was being placed on a leave of absence for the fall term. That meant that he would have to return to a difficult home situation in the tiny rural town of Ewing, Kentucky. Moreover, his father was so opposed to his son's return that he actually decided to move out of the house for the period Chuck would be living at home. "It meant living in a small town with my family where I would get very negative messages: I was gay, I had a mental illness, I was some sicko," he says. But he had no choice; once again, the hospital wouldn't release him without a place to go and home seemed better than staying in the hospital for months.

At home he found a doctor who immediately put him on Prozac, whereupon he rapidly improved. "It became absolutely clear to me," he says, "that if I had been on medication all along, it would have been enormously helpful." He has recently petitioned to return to school for the spring semester, and he is waiting to hear the results.

He recalls how, when he was considering going to Harvard, he asked the interviewer about Harvard's reputation as a big impersonal school which cares more about research and fund raising than undergraduates. The interviewer assured him that the reputation was completely false and gave him a lot of literature which characterized Harvard as caring and attentive. Chuck still believes Harvard has a great deal to offer academically, but in terms of his personal life and problems, he is certain he would have been much better off at a smaller school.

At the end of the summer of 1996, when he was waiting to see whether he was going to be allowed to return to Harvard, he mentioned to a senior Harvard official, who was overseeing his case, that he had been contacted by me about an interview. The official told him the administration did not like students talking to reporters, and that were he to do so the university would not look favorably on his status. He felt intimidated, as he very much wanted to return to school, but he ultimately decided it was important to talk because "the longer they go on being like that, the more students will get hurt."

What seems most damaging about the attitude Harvard adopted is that Chuck's depression, with its suicidal manifestation, was treated not as an illness but as an *infraction*—one subject to disciplinary action. "A suicide attempt means it's suddenly a question whether you're allowed to be in school—and you're guilty until proven innocent. At this time you're feeling badly about yourself, you have to put all your energy into dealing with their condemnation."

Seth Mnookin, class of '94, developed a debilitating problem at college for which Harvard did not support his efforts to get treatment because they refused to accept that it was a medical problem: a drug habit.

In an article he published in *The Harvard Crimson* titled, "Harvard Advising Is a Disgrace," Seth writes that, having grown up locally and having lived on his own before college, he had not expected Harvard to be much of a transition. Moreover, he writes, he had "no illusions about my intellectual ability and thereby avoided unnecessary crises of faith." His freshman-year roommate, however, a valedictorian from Dallas, suffering from a genius complex, began sleeping all day, wandering along the Charles River at night, bringing back homeless guests to their room. Seth talked to several administrators about transferring rooms but his requests were denied. It was not until second semester, when his roommate was throwing empty liquor bottles against the wall and Seth was desperate—unable to work or sleep and turning to drugs—that he was finally allowed to move. His roommate was left alone in their room, where he received no help and ended up leaving school during finals, having failed all his courses.

The drug habit Seth had developed freshman year continued during his sophomore year, and by Thanksgiving break he made the decision to seek treatment at McLean inpatient drug treatment center. "This time," he writes, "I knew not to look to Mother Harvard," so he had made the arrangements himself and then informed his senior tutor he would be entering McLean and was not sure whether he would be back that semester.

Four days into his stay in the hospital, Seth's senior tutor called him. Although Harvard allows students to withdraw midsemester for medical reasons and return automatically the following semester, the Harvard Ad Board—unlike the American Medical Association and the American Psychiatric Association—did not consider drug addiction a medical condition. Seth was told that, if he didn't want to be forced to take spring semester off as well, he would have to return to his classes by the end of the week. His senior tutor believed all he needed to do was get back to work and discipline himself; letters from numerous doctors made no difference.

He returned to school and continued to be plagued by drug problems—problems he combated for many years, returning to inpatient facilities twice and being treated at a handful of outpatient facilities. He recalls once bumping into his senior tutor in the dining hall, a year after the original incident, and without asking him how he was, or even whether he was sober, she smiled at him and said, "See, it turns out we made the right decision after all."

Seth writes that "the underlying reality is that Harvard expects its students to be the best and the brightest and the most well adjusted . . . the rule can be more or less summed up as sink or swim." He thinks that Harvard needs to start paying attention to "its student body's collective emotional state and realize that Harvard students might need some help in their emotional lives even if they are perfect in every other way."

The mismanagement of students suffering from psychological problems and mental illness is hardly unique to Harvard. Dr. Margaret Chisolm, a former psychiatrist at the student counseling center and faculty member of the School of Medicine at Johns Hopkins, says that the student health service at Johns Hopkins is "very inadequate to treat psychiatric illness." Students are seen once initially and sorted into short-term and long-term patients. Long-term patients—personality disorders, eating disorders, or any kind of major mental illness—are referred out—a policy, she says, which "doesn't work because there is no place to refer them to. Students have financial and transportation barriers and the community mental health service which treats indigents is very sub-optimal. In general, when we identify students who are seriously ill we are pressured to give them a medical diagnosis which recommends withdrawal, which is often not in the students' best interest."

Dr. Chisolm thinks "the sickest people should be treated *on campus*. Even just as a matter of risk management this makes the most sense." As had been true at UHS, the counseling center at Johns Hopkins had once provided long-term psychotherapy. However, five years ago it was reorganized to be more cost effective and to try to treat the greatest number of students for minor problems, rather than a smaller number who had major problems. It is a policy, Dr. Chisolm said, that suits the staff, most of whom "chose to work in a student health service because they're interested in noncrisis counseling—problems of adjustment. Most of the people who work there see things from a developmental model, but the number one problem students come in with is depression, which is a medical condition." She says that the staff often seemed "surprised by the severity of problems. But there's no correlation between intellect and mental health. One sees 4.0 students—students on their way to top medical schools who are cutting their genitals at night.

"It's a policy of putting your head in the sand which just doesn't work, given the number of students I saw who had homicidal or suicidal ideation," she said. "My main concern has always been that there would be a suicide or homicide because of a failure of care—because our services are lacking. When I read about the Harvard murder my very first thought was that this could happen here—and that something better change or it will. And then it did."

On April 10, 1996, Robert J. Harwood, Jr., fatally shot Rex T. Chao, a former friend with whom he had had an intense relationship, as Chao was walking on the Johns Hopkins campus with his girlfriend. The murder was the culmination of a long series of events. Chao had broken off his relationship with Harwood late the previous winter, to which Harwood responded with a series of harassing phone calls and E-mail messages. Both students had complained to university officials and a series of meetings had ensued in which questions were discussed such as whether Harwood had a First Amendment right to bring a gun on campus. Finally officials had brokered an agreement, by which Harwood would notify officials before he entered campus—which he had done the day he shot Chao. (Harwood was living in Rhode Island at the time of the murder, having completed his course work and waiting for May graduation.) Chao had been concerned enough by the threats to have hired a lawyer.

Dr. Chisolm says that there is a pattern at Johns Hopkins in which "behavior is treated as a disciplinary problem when it is actually a psychological problem." She has seen several instances in which "students were put through sexual harassment programs which did not include psychiatric counseling and failed because the perpetrator was psychotic." In this case, she says, "the dean of students had met with the perpetrator and the victim eight times before the murder occurred. In none of that time did it occur to her—or was there a university policy—that the harasser get a psychiatric evaluation at student services." Harwood is now in jail, his lawyer preparing an insanity defense.

Just as UHS did, Dr. Chisolm says, "the health service did a stellar job of crisis counseling after it was too late. Once these things happen, there's nothing you can do about it afterward. The victim's family is ravaged, the perpetrator's family is ravaged, there is no possible reparation." Moreover, she says, "the self-scrutiny by the university that could lead to improved mental health care for students is eclipsed by the need for protection from blame." She was struck that "one of the main reactions I heard from the counselors at the health service was 'Thank God we never saw him here'—that is, 'Thank God, we didn't have to see anyone who is really sick'—whereas [her] reaction was 'How terrible we didn't see him because we might have been able to help.' "

She thinks mental illness is an enduring reality on campus.

"There's no way an admissions committee can screen out mentally ill students—they are going to be part of the population and they have to be treated. The late teens and early twenties is the time of onset of the major mental illnesses."

D r. Paul R. McHugh, director of the Department of Psychiatry at the Johns Hopkins School of Medicine, has been campaigning for changes in the student counseling center for years. After the Chao murder he wrote a forceful memo to the student counseling service outlining his concerns, in which he states that a meaningful proportion of students coming to the student counseling center suffer from a mental illness—particularly an affective disorder like depression. As 1.5 percent of the general population suffers from depression in a given year, a university population of 7,000 students should expect to see 105 afflicted students per year. Among these patients, he writes, 15–20 percent are likely to be severely disturbed and suicidal, which means the health service will have fifteen to twenty very sick students—a nontrivial number.

He sees the pattern of undertreatment in student health services as "a reflection of the age-old problem that the culture of mental health is not treated like other sicknesses." A student would never go into a health service for another medical condition, such as asthma, and be told they can be seen for six visits and after that they can drown in their own sputum. Yet limiting the number of visits is common in student mental health services across the country. Dr. McHugh's memo states that "the students in university counseling services are poorly served, in ways that would not be tolerated if they were seeking health service assistance for such medical problems as epilepsy or peptic ulcer. Depression is treated differently and it should not be because like those conditions it has a chronic aspect and a treatment protocol." The argument that depression is different from other medical conditions because its nature is more ambiguous is not valid, he says; neuroscience is closing in on the genetics and pathology of depression, just as it has with other diseases. Following a medical model, patients should be expected to improve over time, he says, and if they don't, regular reevaluations of the diagnosis and treatment are needed.

Colleges often feel insufficient pressure to improve their mental health services because a poor mental health service is not regarded as a significant disadvantage in a college. For example, students choosing between Harvard and Yale would be unlikely to consider that—in part because it has a clinical psychology program—Yale offers much more extensive psychological services. Yet just as in the case of other serious medical problems, when a student becomes mentally ill during his or her time in college, the extent and quality of those services becomes critical.

Dr. McHugh says that he has been "complaining about this for twenty years," but the counselors at Johns Hopkins have an "ideological opposition to medicalization," and a commitment to what he calls "the life-story approach"—the idea that mental disorders are all due to adjustment problems, whose roots lie in unresolved childhood conflicts. The counselors at Johns Hopkins, he says, subscribe to the belief that "category defines condition." Just as elderly people are all presumed to have dementia, so college students are all presumed to be suffering from adjustment problems relating to their self-esteem, competition, absence from home, etc. And many of the students they see *are* simply suffering from those problems, but a few are suffering from something qualitatively different: an illness of neurotransmitters, which needs to be treated by a doctor with medication, as well as intensive psychotherapy.

He believes that all students coming into the health service need to be given an initial thorough screening and psychiatric evaluation to distinguish the mentally ill students from the others. He feels this is a critical step because students like Damian Schloming who suffer from a manic-depressive illness will not get better with Benedryl and warm milk, and a "false negative" diagnostic error can lead to disaster. Depression is associated with high mortality; up to a fifth of those severly afflicted die by suicide.

He has found that the counselors at Johns Hopkins have a deep resistance to the very notion of a psychiatric evaluation, which they feel is not necessary to do therapy. "Can you imagine," he says, "if we had surgeons who said, 'I'm just trained to cut'? I'm fit to be tied about our murder here because the student was never evaluated."

A ccording to Dr. Catlin, Sinedu was seen only by Dr. Powell, a part-time employee of the health service, whose only listed degree is an Ed.D. from the Harvard School of Education—which does not have a clinical psychology program. He also runs a successful college counseling and psychological testing service, Powell Associates, and he is the author of a guide for parents, *Teenagers: When to Worry and What to Do,* in which he created a color-coded system to identify danger signs in adolescents. In the preface to the book Dr. Powell states that he has had a "long interest in understanding the differences among normal adolescents, one passing through temporary difficulties and another in serious trouble." The book lists criteria to distinguish the "qualities separating the green and yellow zones of lesser concern from the orange and red of more pathological conditions." The orange and red zones list danger signs such as: "Intellectualization Inhibiting Enjoyment," "Isolation from Age-mates," "Disaffection, Withdrawal, Depression," "Distorted Negative Thinking," "Recurring Suicidal Thoughts and Talk,"

"Chronic Pain and Unhappiness," "Setting of Unrealistically High Goals," and "Feelings of Emptiness."

In a meeting with Sinedu's cousins and Neb the morning of her death, Dr. Powell told them he had seen Sinedu shortly before she died, and had been trying to reach her on Saturday to cancel an appointment for Monday. He knew she had been having roommate problems, he said, but he had had no idea this would happen, and her problems hadn't seemed like anything out of the ordinary. But he also said he couldn't answer any questions because her therapy was confidential, even after death.

Neither Sinedu's family nor the Ho family nor the district attorney's office have ever seen Sinedu's psychiatric records. Most states, including Massachusetts, have laws mandating that if a patient specifically targets someone and poses a danger to that person, the therapist has an obligation to override confidentiality in order to warn the potential victim, report to the police, and commit the patient to a hospital for observation. These rulings followed in the wake of the 1969 case of Tanya Tarasoff, a nineteen-year-old college student at the University of California Berkeley, who was murdered by Prosenjit Poddar, a twenty-five-year-old Indian graduate student. He had developed an obsessive love for her and had confided his plans to kill her to both a friend and two therapists at the student health service over a period of many months.

If Sinedu had confided her homicidal fantasies to Dr. Powell, as she did in her journals, Harvard could be liable to the Ho family. In order to obtain Sinedu's psychiatric records, though, the Ho family would have to subpoena them, which they could only do by filing a lawsuit—a long, expensive process—and even then the records might remain protected by the psychotherapist–patient privilege. (In the event of a lawsuit, moreover, Harvard's liability is limited to $20,000 in accordance with its mysterious status as a charitable institution.)

Assistant District Attorney Martin Murphy said that his office interviewed Dr. Powell, who told them that Sinedu had not expressed homicidal desires or plans. However, Mr. Murphy said, his office did not have access to Sinedu's psychiatric records to confirm whether or not that was true.

The idea that Dr. Powell might have noticed nothing wrong with Sinedu is a disturbing one. Dr. McHugh, who reviewed Sinedu's diaries and letters, including a letter Sinedu wrote Dr. Powell, commented: "If they had brought Sinedu in and had her seen by a psychiatrist for an initial evaluation, it would stand everyone in good stead, even if a horrible murder had happened." In most states only doctors who possess an M.D., a Ph.D. in psychology, or a Psy.D. are legally allowed to make psychiatric diagnoses—not those with an Ed.D. like Dr. Powell, because, Dr. McHugh says, "a degree in education does not provide sufficient training in the evaluation of mental illness.

"What is shocking to me," Dr. McHugh says, "is that even after the murder, instead of having a medical diagnosis, you have Dr. Catlin giving you a life-story perspective—about how Sinedu must have had narrowly based self-esteem and become overly dependent on someone who rejected her. It's a good story, but how many people is that true of? It sounds like a story Dr. Catlin likes to tell. A Bürgermeister can tell stories; a student who is ill needs a physician. From the letter Sinedu wrote to Dr. Powell, it is clear she was close to being delusionally depressed," he says.

Sinedu's letter to Dr. Powell contains what seem like classical descriptions of clinical depression and its seductive solipsism. She writes that she "can't stand the bright light outside my shell," but she also realizes that she is "debilitated and made lifeless by the comforting darkness of my shell." Yet, she says, she only feels "secure" when she is back in her "dear bed, back to my loneliness, away from the eyes of others." She talks about the loss of concentration characteristic of clinical depression: "When you hung alone so much you tend to forget things a lot. Your memory rusts." Plaintively she asks why she has to be the one "to suffer out of five billion people."

Dr. McHugh says that he "showed the letter to the director of our affective disorders clinic at Johns Hopkins, without telling him who wrote it, and asked what he made of it. He said: 'You're joking, this clearly seems like someone suffering from a major depressive disorder—bring her in for treatment immediately.' " With the revolution in antidepressant medication, depression is the most treatable of mental illnesses; according to the National Institute of Mental Health, treatment of clinical depression is eighty percent to ninety percent successful.

Sinedu writes to Dr. Powell that if he is to remain her doctor she really needs to meet with him more frequently. She begins by telling him that it has been a "very very long time since I last saw you. To you, I am only one of your subjects, but to me, you are my last hope and my last chance." She tries to hold on between appointments, she writes, but she can't. In her letter to the stranger Sinedu writes that her therapist is very busy and can only see her once a month, or once a fortnight—not enough therapy to treat someone as ill as Sinedu, especially without medication.

In her letter to the stranger, Sinedu writes, "I write a lot of diaries . . . [but] the one help that I believe and have always believed would be very crucial for my success is someone who will constantly check in on me & share both the good and bad part of my life with me." It is clear, however, that Sinedu was sufficiently disturbed that no friendship could have met her needs: the relationship she was longing for could only have been one with a therapist. She fixated on Trang's rejection, but had she actually been able to make use of a friendship, there were people available to her. She had her cousins and most significantly Neb, who cared for her and had no idea why she never confided in him.

Susan Besharov, a Washington, D.C., based clinical social worker who reviewed Sinedu's diaries, says that "what makes Sinedu seem so ripe for treatment is that she does have a good deal of insight. She is able to make connections to her early childhood experience. She also takes an impressive responsibility for her problems, rather than just externalizing or blaming the world. What is so poignant for me as a therapist about Sinedu's diaries is that she is both so acutely aware of her depression and is working terribly hard to compensate for her emotional deficits. This is what makes her therapy—with its infrequency and lack of medication—seem like such a missed opportunity."

During a depressive illness (which is twice as likely to affect women as men) sufferers are overcome by a radical, unshakable negative view of themselves and the world—a fog so thick they are unable to see the world as they had previously experienced it. An episode of major depression can last for a period of weeks up to several years, but the average runs its course in six to nine months, although in some patients it never fully remits, and for many it is a recurrent phenomenon. Its symptoms include feelings of worthlessness, guilt, hopelessness, and weariness; difficulty thinking, concentrating, or making decisions; recurrent thoughts of death and suicidal plans or attempts.

The defining quality of clinical depression, however, is not its negativity but its *unrealistic* negativity. A depressed person's self-description is usually at odds with the external evidence—a banker may complain of poverty, but when his psychiatrist consults with the patient's wife, it becomes clear he is suffering not from financial hardship but from depression.

Many of Sinedu's descriptions of her problems, on the other

hand, seem *realistic:* she felt she had great difficulty connecting with other people and this seems to be true. While she doubtless did have a mood disorder, Sinedu's problems—her lifelong interpersonal difficulties—seem to have been of the variety psychologists call a personality disorder.

P ersonality disorders are defined by the DSM-IV (the standard diagnostic manual of mental disorders) as "maladaptive personality traits: enduring patterns of inner experience and behavior that are pervasive and inflexible, and lead to distress or impairment," affecting a wide range of functions including "cognition, affectivity, interpersonal functioning, and impulse control." While depression primarily describes the way individuals feel about themselves, personality disorders describe the way others feel about them—the individuals' relationship to the world, of which self-image is only a part.

The DSM-IV lists ten recognized personality disorders. While postmortem diagnoses are always problemetic, a number of mental health professionals with whom I consulted felt that, to the extent to which they could evaluate Sinedu based on her writings, she seemed to display traits from several categories.

Paranoid Personality Disorder involves a pattern of distrust and suspicion such that others' motives are interpreted as malevolent. Avoidant Personality Disorder is a pattern of social inhibition, feelings of inadequacy, and hypersensitivity to negative evaluation. Obsessive Compulsive Personality Disorder is a pattern of preoccupation with orderliness, perfectionism, and control. Borderline Personality Disorder is a pattern of marked instability in interpersonal relationships, self-image, and affects—fluctuating between idealization and devaluation of other people, often showing intense, inappropriate anger, feeling empty or bored, and frantic efforts to avoid real or imagined abandonment.

Although Sinedu clearly has elements from all of these, the diagnosis therapists agree fit her best is the Schizotypal Personality Disorder: a pervasive pattern of social and interpersonal deficits marked by acute discomfort with and reduced capacities for close relationships, as well as by cognitive or perceptual distortions and eccentricities of behavior. The DSM-IV defines Schizotypal Personality Disorder as follows:

> Individuals often have ideas of reference (i.e. incorrect interpretations of casual incidents and external events as having a particular and unusual meaning specifically for that person). . . . These individuals may be superstitious . . . they may feel they have special powers . . . or magical control over others. . . . Their speech may include unusual or idiosyncratic phrasing or construction. It is often loose, digressive, or vague. . . . Responses can be overly concrete or overly abstract, or words or concepts are sometimes applied in unusual ways (e.g. the person may state that he or she was not "talkable" at work.)
>
> Individuals with this disorder are often suspicious and may have paranoid ideation. . . . They are usually not able to negotiate the full range of affects and interpersonal cueing required for successful relationships and thus often appear to interact with others in an inappropriate, stiff or constricted fashion. . . .
>
> Although they may express unhappiness about their lack of relationships, their behavior suggests a decreased desire for intimate contacts. As a result, they usually have few or no close friends or confidants. . . . They are anxious in social

situations, particularly those involving unfamiliar people.
. . . Their social anxiety does not easily abate, even when
they spend more time in the setting or become more familiar
with other people because their anxiety tends to be associated
with suspiciousness regarding others' motivations. . . .

Particularly in response to stress, individuals with this
disorder may experience transient psychotic episodes (lasting
minutes to hours). . . . From 30% to 50% of individuals with
this disorder have a concurrent diagnosis of Major Depressive
Disorder. . . . There is considerable co-occurrence with
Schizoid, Paranoid, Avoidant and Borderline Personality Disorders. . . .

Schizotypal Personality Disorder may first be apparent in
childhood and adolescence with solitariness, poor peer relationships, social anxiety . . . peculiar thoughts and language
and bizarre fantasies. These children may appear "odd," or
"eccentric," and attract teasing.

Several aspects of the description seem to resonate with Sinedu.
She lacked what the DSM-IV describes as the "interpersonal cueing
required for successful relationships"—a lack of which she was pain-
fully aware (writing that from earliest childhood she felt other girls had
"some kind of sixth sense that I was foreign to"). She "often appear[s]
to interact with others in an inappropriate, stiff or constricted fashion"—the stiff, robotic quality people recall about her and which she
writes about in her journals, expressing fear of inappropriate responses, which she tries to monitor through rules. ("Put on a mask. If
you are talking about something serious, make your face serious. If you
want to threaten, put away your smile and look ominous.")

The language of Sinedu's journals is notably strange—a strange-
ness that cannot be accounted for by her foreignness, as Ethiopians

who have reviewed them find the writing peculiar. English was, after all, the language of her schooling all her life, and the papers she wrote for Harvard classes are technically proficient and her verbal SAT scores high. But in her diaries the prose seems adapted to her internal world. Her language is both overly concrete and overly abstract, in a way that seems not to reflect so much a poverty of language as one of mind—as if, while she is desperately trying to interpret her world, she is looking through the wrong end of the telescope and the picture that emerges is distant and distorted—a distance she is aware of but unable to readjust.

She often employs odd compound words and images. She describes her feelings of disconnection from others as "this heart-failer thing," her freshman roommate as having "pranked over" her prostrated body, her desire to "illude to myself as reaping friends like wheat." Her imagery is bizarre: in the passage where she writes that the bad way out is "suicide & the good way out killing & then suicide," she writes that what keeps her from acting on her murderous desires is the feeling of being "both hand & leg-cuffed to a couch stuck in the ground." And then she adds, as if by way of explanation: "Sometimes even if a bomb falls beside me, I would be scared at first and then not even bother to see what happened."

The internal connection between these images is oblique: we presume the couch she is handcuffed to (perhaps a therapist's couch) is depression, the bomb (perhaps an allusion to war trauma) her murderous rage, and her indifference ("not even bother") to her internal state a description of the apathy of depression which makes it likely that the bomb will go off. The imagery, however, seems uncontrolled and dreamlike—as if the writer is not fully cognizant of what she is writing. The use of the passive tense seems to reflect deep confusion on the question of agency: she is chained, a bomb is falling, she wants to commit murder, but she doesn't know if she can.

Some of her writings contain what the DSM-IV calls "ideas of reference," in particular the belief, at times, that she is in possession of special powers or magical control over others—a fantasy whose collapse she experiences with despair. ("There is no power that lies in me that I could use however I want to. I am unable to make friends. There is no magic I control.") But it is a psychopathology she finally succumbed to, seizing the one absolute power a human ever has over another: the power to kill.

Personality disorders are considered especially difficult to treat because in some sense they "work" for the person. While sufferers function at a chronically impaired level, their behavior often represents a stable psychic construct. Individuals suffering from Schizotypal Personality Disorder are generally outcasts, but they have adapted emotionally to their social deficiencies, such that they often do not experience a desire for close relationships. Sinedu, however, possessed a keen—indeed a desperate—longing for relationships, and her intense unhappiness with a personality she felt incapable of changing propelled her toward fatal action.

The origin of personality disorders is mysterious. In her letter to the stranger Sinedu writes of her puzzlement as to the source of her problems: "My parents did not beat or abuse me . . . as a result I was unable to point to any tangible cause." But in another place, in a poemlike format, she writes a series of thirty-three questions about her background, asking whether anyone had ever made her feel special, loved, comforted; inspired trust or admiration; offered wisdom; or taught her how to be "sweet"? Each question is written out in a different line, followed by a line with the answer—an unvarying refrain of "No." Her letter to the stranger focuses on the emotional deprivations of her childhood:

> I have been raised in what you might be able to call an abnormal situation. I don't understand what people mean by the warmth of a family, the love of their mother and the security of their home. I grew up feeling lonely and cold amidst two parents and four siblings. I had no one to rely on for warmth. . . . I failed to make friends over the years. I spent very little time with other families that it took me all my life to figure out what they had & what I did not have. My parents were shy & lonely. They kept away from the world. . . . They did not want to face their problems. They pre-tended as if nothing was wrong. They fed us, bought us clothes, sent us to good schools & wished us all the best. They never involved themselves in our emotional world. They acted as if emotions did not exist.

Most psychiatrists, however, now believe that a key component in mental illness is a biological vulnerability. While Sinedu's childhood was clearly not "good enough" for her, it may well have been good enough for someone with a different biopsychic makeup, and indeed it was apparently adequate for her siblings—none of whom became murderers. (For that matter, Trang's childhood involved hardship, but that hardship seems to have strengthened rather than damaged her.)

Included in Sinedu's journals are several pages labeled "Case History to tell Dr. Powell." In that, as well as in her letter to the stranger, Sinedu describes how the family was plunged into "the most chaotic life ever" during her father's two-year imprisonment beginning when she was seven and a half. Her mother had to work as a nurse until eight o'clock every night, while the children had to stay late at school because there was no one to pick them up. There was a constant turnover of the servants and the children frequently had to do all the housework themselves. "My hands and legs became coarse because there was no cream or vaseline," she writes in her letter to the stranger. "Meals were bland, just to have something in the stomach. Breakfast was plain bread and tea because we couldn't afford milk. I had to go to school with worn-out shoes and clothes."

With her father gone, Sinedu was left alone with the mother whom she "hated" and "really really believed hated me." She writes that her mother had a compulsion to "kill" herself with work—coming home at night to redo the maids' work, claiming it had not been done properly, remopping the stone floors, supervising the preparation of the grains to make *injira*, hand-washing the laundry. On weekends, to Sinedu's shame, her mother would actually go out with an ax and cut down tree trunks for firewood.

Sinedu writes that she would occasionally feel guilt at seeing her mother labor, but trying to help her was a Sisyphean task: one could never do enough and what one did would always be subject to harsh criticism. Sinedu describes how her mother would "nag" Sinedu and her siblings "to death," attacking them brutally for small mistakes, like spilling a cup of milk, and berating them with endless rules—a harsh critical voice perhaps very much like the one Sinedu addresses to herself in her Rule Book.

But Sinedu is also very aware of her own similarity to the mother she describes hating so much: she sees herself as a workaholic, angry and depressed. In her letter to the stranger Sinedu writes: "If I live I do not want to live like my mother—lonely and sad." She describes her mother as never having had close friends, and as alienating her father's friends and all their relatives.

Sinedu's birth had coincided with the military coup of the Derg regime. When she was two years old the Red Terror began: a disaster for the country and a personal disaster for Sinedu's family as well, who as upper-class Amhara had lost the emperor's protection and were now at the gravest risk. Sinedu's mother would certainly have had significant reason to be preoccupied, fearful, and unhappy during the formative years of Sinedu's childhood, as well as distracted by the four other children she had to tend to.

Sinedu seems to have internalized some notion of responsibility for the family misfortune—an idea she knows logically is false and tries to talk herself out of in her journals, but which seems to have persistent psychological resonance. One of her diary rules is never to mention to people at Harvard that she was born in the year that the emperor fell because—although she knows it's not her fault—others might misunderstand and think that she regrets her birth or associates it with disaster.

With the outside world a place of war, famine, and political repression, Sinedu's family remained locked into itself. Ethiopians often attribute their ability to survive the adversities of their history to the strength of their extended families and communities. "You cannot have a bad family in Ethiopia," Tizita Belachew, an Ethiopian refugee and a broadcaster for the Voice of America International, says. "Families are very big. Children have many mothers—relatives and neighbors. The whole neighborhood is a family." During Sinedu's father's imprisonment, however, Sinedu's mother cut off all their relatives, declaring them all "snakes." She told the children that their father's friends were "wicked" and had betrayed him to the government and that everyone outside their family was "selfish, shrewd, and cunning." There was constant "political torture fear," and the children were told not to trust anyone outside the family—"no one at all." Sinedu writes that it would actually surprise her when on a rare occasion she encountered someone outside the family and realized that the person didn't wish them harm.

Interpreting the characters of individuals based on the historical events that surrounded them is always tricky; certainly not everyone growing up during the Red Terror turned out to have similar psychological profiles. But many of Sinedu's perceptions do seem to reflect having come of age in a society in which the murderers have the power. Psychologists often talk about the developmental importance of outside influences to correct for the distortions of the family. But the world during the Derg regime only reinforced what seemed to have been the particular pathologies of Sinedu's family. Sinedu's mother may have been communicating paranoia to her children, but during a time in which neighbors, friends, and servants were betraying one another to the secret police, there was reason to be paranoid.

Moreover, there is no convention in Ethiopia of discussing family problems with outsiders. As Bethlehem Gelaw, a classmate of Sinedu's from ICS, says, "I never knew Sinedu didn't have a warm family. The things she says about her family are not shocking by American standards, where family connections are often broken, but they are very shocking by Ethiopian standards. In Ethiopia, family is everything."

Sinedu's father returned from prison a ruined man. His job as headmaster of government schools was not restored to him. Soon after, he retired and the family struggled to survive on Sinedu's mother's salary. As a child, Sinedu had been proud that her father was educated and well dressed, but after he got out of prison, in accordance with communist ideology, he changed his style to imitate a traditional Ethiopian man, dressing in peasant garb she "despised" and felt humiliated by. The house deteriorated and there was no money for repairs. She writes that she was so "totally ashamed" of the state of the house and its lack of modern electronics—particularly a tape recorder, which she saw as "the 1st necessity," for entertaining—that she would never bring friends home from school.

Her parents' marriage appeared to Sinedu loveless and combative. In her letter to the stranger she writes:

All this time I blamed lack of money as a cause to all my troubles. But somewhere deep inside me I knew money would not have been all the answer to my problems, although life would have been better with money. I saw the answer in my parents. As long as I knew her, my mother never had a friend or close relatives. She avoided social occasions and kept herself busy with housework. We never had warm family days because all conversation was tainted with the irritating argument between my parents. They had nothing to talk about so they picked on each other and on us. Political problems, civil wars, and the ever increasing price of goods took care of conversation at dinner time from day to day. I never felt proud of my family. As a matter of fact, I never admired or respected myself.

What my parents did not do for me was, they did not give me love, they did not make me feel important in their lives, they did not guide me in social life. They always told me & my siblings how other kids are much better than we are. They did not make friends. They did not enjoy their lives. They nagged at us; they quarreled, abused us emotionally.

There was no comfort to seek from them, no warmth. Life was cold & hopeless & annoying. Do not get me wrong, I do not blame them for all they did; they did not know how else to be. They repeated their parents' history. I don't want to be a third generation of misfits.

Although she knew her siblings were also suffering, Sinedu writes that none of them helped one another. She describes how during puberty, her brother and sister began mercilessly mocking her appearance—calling her big-bottomed, big-headed, and huge. Her father's friend used to call her "very black," and her mother used to tease her about being a "no-nose,"—common Ethiopian insults (light skin color and a prominent well-defined nose are standards of Ethiopian beauty). She felt, however, that her siblings' teasing had a more malicious damaging spirit. Of course it was true that she wasn't pretty, she writes, but she thinks that her family should have loved her in spite of her appearance.

It was during the time of her father's imprisonment that Sinedu first sought refuge in what she describes as the "the worst of all habits": obsessive fantasizing. She began to spend hours daydreaming about herself as a happy, wealthy student living in a happy, wealthy family—fantasies so powerful she had trouble distinguishing them from reality. She recalls a delusional moment when she was ten or eleven, during which she actually wrote a good-bye note to her family so that she could go live with her fantasy family and then waited for God to transport her. Meanwhile she continued to slave at her schoolwork during the day in order to win the scholarship that would take her to America.

———

J ust as she had once conjured a perfect imaginary family for herself in Ethiopia, after the initial disappointment of Harvard, Sinedu began to fantasize about an ideal friend who would solve the same host of problems. It is interesting to speculate how she alighted on Trang to fill that role. She was probably drawn to Trang less for their apparent similarities and more for the emotional resources she saw in Trang, and which she knew she was lacking. Sinedu could see that Trang functioned as a caretaker for those she was close to: her mother, her sisters, and her friend Thao. From the moment Trang agreed to live with her, Sinedu made her the "Queen" of her life—the object of all of her hopes for love, nurturing, and dominance.

Unfortunately, relationships involving a great deal of so-called projection are rarely successful. One might imagine that a maternally deprived person such as Sinedu might project those longings to an adult relationship and actually succeed in having those needs met. Instead, the projection usually works to transform the other person not into the imaginary longed-for parent but into a psychic replica of the true unsatisfactory parent, replaying the same process of disappointment, disillusionment, and rage. When Sinedu's hopes in Trang were dashed, she was flooded with familiar depression and thirst for vengeance.

Revenge is often a dominant motif in suicide and murder/suicide. Studies of completed suicides, using psychiatric records and suicide notes, indicate that the desire for revenge (although the wish to kill is turned upon oneself) is a primary motive in half of all suicides.[3] In the part of her journals she calls her "Case History," Sinedu writes of her resolution to get even with her mother one day for her ill-treatment ("wait until I show her. She will regret for treating me badly").

Studies of homicide/suicides show that half to three quarters involve the desire for a more specific kind of revenge: what sociologists refer to as "amorous jealousy"—also known as psychotic or morbid jealousy. The typical murder/suicide is one in which a male is suspicious of a lover's infidelity, becomes enraged, and murders his lover and himself. The triggering event is often the female's rejection of her lover and the threat of the loss or withdrawal of her affections. The "infidelity" may be real or delusional; the delusional psychotic form is actually known as the "Othello Syndrome." Moreover, the betrayal may be done by a real romantic partner, or one who is simply an object of romantic fantasy, as in the 1969 case of Tanya Tarasoff, the Berkeley student murdered by a graduate student who barely knew her.

Homicide/suicide occupies a so-called unique epidemiological domain, different from either homicide or suicide. Careful planning and a very short time span between the killing of the other and self reveals that homicide/suicide is conceived of as a unified plan, in which neither act is incidental to the other. Homicide/suicide differs sociologically from simple homicide in that it is primarily "about" a powerful relationship—ordinarily a romantic or parenting relationship. Whereas the majority of simple homicides involve same-sex disputes over money or drugs, "With few exceptions, virtually all victims of murder/suicide are either female sexual partners or blood relatives, usually children," one study concludes.[4]

Sinedu and Trang were not lovers, but the relationship in Sinedu's mind clearly had elements of a romance. Sinedu's feelings toward Trang seem to have resembled the intense crushlike attachments girls often have for each other—what the psychologist Harry Stack Sullivan calls the "chum," a relationship adults often replace with sexual partners. Sinedu killed Trang when she was in bed with another woman. Ordinarily, the presence of another person would be a *deterrent* from killing; in this case, it may have strengthened her resolve.

For many hours in the early hours of the morning before the killing, Sinedu had lain in bed listening to the queen of her life talking and laughing with someone else, the words—in Vietnamese and English—indistinct, but the tone of intimacy unmistakable, one Sinedu must have recognized with unbearable longing.

When Sinedu was presaging the murder in her letter to *The Crimson,* she described it as a "juicy story"—choosing a word which ordinarily implies sexual scandal, not just tragedy. Sinedu did not simply want Trang dead, she *obliterated* her body, in a physically intimate drawn-out way, with repeated acts of violent penetration. (Stabbing is a male-identified method of killing in Ethiopia—the kind a man might enact on a woman he has caught *in flagrante delicto.* Female-identified methods of murder are witchcraft or poison.)

Nowhere in Sinedu's diaries or in other students' recollections of her did she demonstrate any sexual interest in men. The police suspected that Sinedu had had a romantic relationship with Neb Tilahun, which wasn't true. The suspicion seemed to have stemmed from the fact that in the last week of her life, when she was often seen crying in public places, Sinedu tried to explain away her tears by saying she had just ended a relationship. The police embarked on a long goose chase for a boyfriend who didn't exist; the relationship was, of course, with Trang.

At one point Sinedu writes in her diaries that, although she might "die of loneliness" without a husband, if she ever had one she would be overwhelmed by "shame and guilt." It's hard to know how to interpret this: perhaps Sinedu had some sense of a different sexual orientation. Or perhaps she is referring to feelings of shame often described by Ethiopian women, ninety percent of whom have under-gone ritual female genital mutilation.[5]

I don't know whether Sinedu was mutilated; in reporting this story, I asked questions I would have thought I was incapable of voicing and I was silent at junctures that surprised me—and the subject of ritual genital mutilation was one of those silences. How-ever, the assumption that an Ethiopian woman has been mutilated is as reasonable, an Ethiopian explained to me, as the assumption that an American male has been circumcised: a practice of equivalent preva-lence in our culture. As a result of educational campaigns and interna-tional pressure, female genital mutilation in Ethiopia is beginning to change, but it is still the norm and twenty years ago it was even more so. The practice is particularly strong among members of traditional tribes, like Sinedu's family—Amharas from Menz.

Ritual genital mutilation is performed on women at various ages, from infancy to puberty to the time of marriage. Different forms of the mutilation involve varying degrees of severity, from the clito-ridectomy (the removal of either the hood of the clitoris or the entire clitoris) to excision (the removal of the clitoris and labia minora) to infibulation (the removal of the clitoris and labia minor, after which the two sides of the vulva are sewn together, leaving a small hole for urine and menstrual blood. The orifice is intended to protect virgin-ity; it is supposed to be too small to admit a grain of corn and has to be cut open for intercourse at marriage). Amharas most commonly practice clitoridectomy.

Ethiopian women often describe genital mutilation as their clear-est childhood memory: being immobilized, often without warning or anesthetic, and cut with a knife, razor, or sharp piece of glass by a gang of women that includes their own mothers. In addition to the initial trauma of the ritual, Ethiopian women often now have the additional trauma of learning—as the result of recent educational reforms—that their bodies have been disfigured and they will never experience full sexual pleasure. A woman in Ethiopia told me how her husband had slept with a prostitute who had not been mutilated, and then told her that she was "like dead wood down there." An Ethiopian immigrant described to me her fear of dating Western men because of the paralyzing anxiety that they would reject a body that must strike them as profoundly disfigured.

The development of a psychotic jealousy—the belief that Trang's rejection was a fatal blow, unsurvivable and punishable by death—apparently happened in a relatively short period of time, during the last week of Sinedu's life. Her diaries reflect a deep, perhaps even a psychotic depression, but psychotic depressions are usually sufficiently incapacitating that the person is not capable of violence. In the passage in which Sinedu urges herself to take the "good solution" of killing, she says her depression is as paralyzing as being handcuffed, leaving her able to do "nothing." And, in fact, she did do "nothing" for almost two years after first formulating the idea—and then, during the last week of term, she suddenly began to make plans.

Although a definite diagnosis cannot be made and other mental illnesses such as the onset of schizophrenia cannot be ruled out, several psychiatrists have speculated that Sinedu may have had a manic episode at the end of her life. Five to ten percent of individuals suffering from major depression subsequently develop a manic episode, the medium age of onset of which is twenty-one. According to the DSM-IV: "The acute onset of severe depression, especially with psychotic features and psychomotor retardation, in a young person . . . is more likely to predict a bipolar course."

During manic episodes individuals are imbued with feelings of omnipotence and frantic sleepless elation. But although these feelings often result in foolish or self-destructive gestures, they do not often lead to violence because the person is feeling "good." During a mixed mania, however—a particularly dangerous kind of mania— individuals exhibit both manic and depressive symptoms. They thus have the energy to act on their misery, as it were: the feelings of omnipotence along with the deluded desperation of depression.

In the final week of her life Sinedu bought two knives and some rope, sent a notice to *The Crimson*, and arranged to say good-bye to Neb. When Neb met with her, he was struck by her mood of giddy elation, the "happiest" he had ever seen her. He was also struck by what was—by her previous standards—inappropriately sexualized dress: a characteristic sign of mania. But she was depressed that week as well; she was seen crying and unable to concentrate on her studies. The last weekend she appeared to sleep little. When Trang went out Saturday morning, Sinedu was hunched on the bed, in a paralyzed fetal position, her knees up, her head in her hands, crying. When Trang came back into the room that afternoon, she was still in the same position. Saturday night, however, she went to the weight room—for the first time to anyone's knowledge. When Trang and Thao came in from their celebration early Sunday morning, Sinedu was awake, lying on her bed with the light on. In the morning this psychomotor retardation was transformed into the enormous energy with which the crime was executed.

Like most mood-disordered patients contemplating violence, Sinedu displayed ambivalence and the desire for intervention—dyadic "either/or" thinking. She made plans for her death, purchasing a knife and rope, but she also made inquiries about her financial aid for the following year. She got excuses for her first two exams; it wasn't until the final weekend that she was in a frame of mind in which failing a course no longer mattered. On the last day of her life she did a little packing. And when she did kill Trang, it was at the last possible minute: the morning Trang was going to move out of their room permanently, rather than after they had fallen asleep the night before, when it would have been less risky to carry out such a plan. (What if Trang and Thao had decided to get up in the morning when they heard Sinedu's alarm instead of going back to sleep?)

While case conferences about completed suicides and suicide/homicides inevitably reveal the warning signs, they also reveal, psychologists say, that the acts were predictable only in retrospect. "We can tell you a pool of twenty severely depressed patients is at risk for suicide, but we can't tell, ahead of time which one will actually do it," Dr. James Longhurst, a Yale University psychiatrist, tells me. Psychiatric hindsight is twenty-twenty, psychiatrists are fond of saying, but it isn't really, because even in retrospect it is often unclear why those particular patients actually committed the acts. "We can never say why certain patients—rather than other patients with similar or more severe diagnoses—are the ones who actually commit some terrible act," Dr. Longhurst says. "Sinedu's diaries are clearly very disturbed, but they are less disturbed than other patients who don't commit murder and suicide." If she wasn't more disturbed than others all along, then, at some point she crossed over. What caused that crossing? "If you push psychiatrists far enough," Dr. Longhurst says, "you'll find most of them believe in evil."

"I believe in evil," Reverend Peter Gomes told me, standing on the green lawn outside Memorial Chapel a week after the girls' deaths.

"The evil within," I say, "or an evil, out there, a force in the world?"

"An evil which is out there," he says, in his rich ringing preacher's voice, "which surrounds and overwhelms us at times of weakness—in loneliness or war—from which we pray for deliverance."

Assistant District Attorney Martin Murphy says that if Sinedu had lived she would have been charged with first-degree premeditated murder. There would have been a trial, he says, in which the defense would have argued that she was insane and his office would have argued that she wasn't and the jury would have made a decision as to which of those two boxes to put her in.

If she wasn't mentally ill, what was she? What is the second box?

He flounders momentarily. "Bad," he says. He pauses and then adds: "What makes this case seem so mysterious is that the thing which pushed her over—the slight—was so slight."

"Ultimately this is all sad," Dr. Paul McHugh says, "but it's also bad—wrong, sinful, evil. I tell my patients that certain actions are evil actions, and if you do this—if you kill yourself or someone else—I'm going to come after you and drag you out of hell. I say this as a wake-up call to mentally ill patients because I know that when they recover they almost always say: why didn't you keep me from doing this terrible thing? Psychiatrists use the issue of illness to offer forgiveness, and illness does take away some element of choice, but not entirely. If Sinedu had lived she would have asked for forgiveness and we would have explored her illness, but there would have been something I could never take away from her: the fact that something evil did take place, that she played some role in choosing it, and that the losses incurred are irreversible."

S inedu had been buried a month by the time I visited her grave site, on a sloping hillside of a church in Addis Ababa, where goats graze. Suicides are supposed to be buried forty meters from a churchyard, but Sinedu was allowed a Christian burial because the family persuaded the priest that no one really knew what had happened to her. Neb stood a few feet away, his face blank and bewildered, next to Yeshi Tekleab, a teacher from Sinedu's high school, who crossed herself quickly in consternation. On either side of Sinedu were finished graves: long white marble mausoleums, guarded by a cage of iron to keep the marble from being stolen. The head of each mausoleum is inlaid with a small black and white photo of the dead face. Forty days after the burial, Sinedu's gravestone was to be put in: I pictured the familiar photo of her, glimpsed between bars, caught for all time under a swirl of thick glass.

SIX

HALFWAY

HEAVEN

A t the one-year anniversary of Trang's death a Buddhist ceremony is planned to be held at Trang's grave site in Mt. Auburn Cemetery in Cambridge. In the ceremony, a fire is made in a metal bowl and bits of clothing, money, a little house, and letters to the deceased are burned to send to them in heaven. I talk to Thao Nguyen a few weeks before, when she is trying to compose her letter to Trang. She doesn't know what to write; so much has happened in the time that has passed—she has grieved so much for Trang, it has changed her and she doesn't know how to describe that change to Trang.

It is hard to know how to speak to the dead. I recall a leather-bound book on a table at the funeral parlor, just after Trang's death, in which visitors had written notes to the family. Some wrote descriptions of Trang, as if for posterity—noting her smile, her goodness, her blue backpack full of books. Others addressed Trang herself, writing: "I miss you," and "I don't know why you had to die, but good luck in heaven." I looked at the book for a long time but didn't pick up the pen.

A second ceremony is also planned for the anniversary of Trang's death to be held at the Vietnamese Unity Buddhist Temple in Boston. Trang had died on May 28, but her family asks permission of the reverend to have the second ceremony moved to the twenty-sixth, which is the Buddha's birthday, when hundreds of people will be celebrating at the temple and can pray for Trang too. Trang went to the temple often; during her final exams, the last week of her life, she had asked her mother to take her to the temple, but her mother hadn't had time, she recalls now with self-reproach.

The temple was once a Catholic church. It has been repainted red and yellow and the altar has been replaced with a statue of the Sakiyani Buddha, but the stained-glass windows still depict the sufferings of Christ. There is a large table in one corner, crowded with photos of the dead and plates of food which the relatives bring the dead for the first year or two, or longer, if they still miss them too much. The photo of Trang has a schoolgirl purity, shy and confident, her hair brushed straight with bangs, her chin tilted, her gaze upward.

Every week for the first forty-nine days after Trang's death there was a service to pray that her soul will be accepted for salvation by the Buddha and not be reborn on earth again. But even after the first year of mourning ends, the Reverend Dr. Thich Giac Duc prays for Trang every week, as the family asks him to. He tells me that, although it is secret, he can tell through meditation that Trang has entered the Pure Land and has not been reborn. He knows, he says, the way a doctor knows things about people's bodies.

When Trang's grandparents came from Vietnam to see her grave, they had to change planes in a crowded airport in Germany where all the signs were in languages they couldn't read. But they followed something and found their way and then they realized Trang had led them there. If she had been reborn, Dr. Duc explained, she would have moved on to a new life and not been available any longer. But she can still be reached now, called upon to visit and help the people she loves.

A t Trang's funeral her father, Phuoc Xuan Ho, had cried out in Vietnamese, "Don't go, don't go," and "Oh, my dear daughter, you were always smiling. Why did I work so hard for ten years and go through so much in the end if it was all just to bury my daughter?" Having Trang go to Harvard was everything her family had wanted and worked for, a family friend told me, "this beautiful place, which was halfway heaven."

"Harvard will always be in my heart," her father tells me. "For me, it is the best place and the worst place because it is the place where my daughter died."

He places his hope in his youngest child, Tram, now, he says. She is very intelligent, he says; although she has only been in the United States for two years, she is now a student at Tufts. She had planned to study law, but after Trang's death she no longer wanted anything to do with the law. I remember her from the funeral, crying bitterly, a white mourning sash tied around her forehead. She had had a fight with Trang right before she died and now they would never make up. Phuoc says that he thinks his life is hard, but he will try to make it through. He has made it through the war and the camp and losing his country. He remembers proverbs directing one to accept life with a smile, not a tear, no matter how hard.

He has had to struggle in San Diego, with the California recession. The only work he has found is as a technician in a sewing factory, for long hours and little pay. After the divorce, Trang was the one child who always kept in touch with him, signing her sisters' names to her cards. He rereads a card Trang sent him the summer after her high school graduation, when he moved to California alone, a restraining order preventing him from seeing his daughters to say good-bye. "You are always in our heart," she wrote, "even if you're living far away from our family. If you are happy, we are happy." On the opposite page of the card she copied out a saying for him:

> If you love something set it free.
> If it comes back to you, it is yours.
> If it doesn't, it never was.

For the people around her, Trang's death is one in a series of losses. It is part of the double meaning America has always had for them: the country that promised to end the war, but instead entangled them in years of violence, the safe haven they never quite reach. Phuoc thinks that Vietnamese people have a special strength because they have suffered so much—a thousand years under Chinese rule, and then the French, and then the American war, but they have kept their hope and each time they are reborn stronger. He believes that Trang is in a happy place now. Trang worked so hard for happiness and peace her whole life, he says, and now she has both.

Trang's friend Khoi Luu is worried that Trang's mother will look to her past—in this or a previous life—for responsibility for Trang's death. "In Buddhist culture you store up *phuoc*—good karma," he says. "Children inherit the *phuoc*." Khoi's mother always tells him stories of how his grandmother, a wealthy Vietnamese woman, used to save up rice and then during times of famine she would share it with the starving villagers. Khoi's mother believes that that has something to do with why Khoi got into Harvard. "Conversely," he says, "there's an assumption that if things are going badly something must have gone wrong with the ancestors. I hope Trang's mother doesn't think that it's her fault. Women get blamed for everything in Vietnamese culture," he says.

Trang's mother, Quy Huynh, is in a deep depression. She cries constantly and has lost interest in sleeping and cooking and doing housework. She had talked to Trang twice the last day of her life: once in the morning and once at eleven or twelve that night. She had asked Trang to come home after her exam, but Trang had wanted to stay at school the last night and celebrate. During their final phone call, Trang had sounded tired but happy—

they talked about a celebration for Tram's high school graduation and birthday, and Trang said they'd finalize plans the next day, when she got home.

Quy stays home alone all day now, in the small third-floor walkup apartment, praying at a small candlelit shrine for Trang, and wondering what she did wrong in a previous life to deserve to have a daughter die this way. Each morning and evening she sets bowls of rice, vegetables, pastries, and fruit before Trang's photo and burns incense candles, saying prayers and calling Trang's name so the smoke can go up to heaven and tempt Trang's spirit to join them again.

Every landmark is an occasion for sadness: the graduation that should have been Trang's, the start of the fall that would have been her first year in medical school—all the markings of time that leave Trang farther and farther behind. In Vietnamese culture children support their parents; children who let their parents work when they get old don't love them. Even as an undergraduate, Trang had helped pay the rent; as a doctor, she would have provided for them permanently.

The hardest thing, Quy tells me in Vietnamese, is that the family had survived and rebuilt their fortunes after the war, and they decided to come to the States not because they were poor, but because they had three daughters and they wanted them to have opportunities for education and careers that do not exist in their country. "U.S. is supposed to be the land of heaven," she says. "To lose Trang in the U.S. and at school—where you're supposed to go—" She breaks off, crying.

She has great difficulty accepting that Trang is dead. When she misses her she sometimes goes to the Harvard campus and walks around, trying to find her.

Dr. Caitlin told me that the question of Harvard providing continuing counseling for the Ho family was raised at a meeting he attended, but someone raised the inevitable question: "What if they need counseling for the rest of their lives?"

T rang's sister Thao Ho feels very confused about her life. She has dropped out of Tufts, where she was studying biopsychology. She worked in a lab for a while, but she is now unemployed. She feels she has to stanch the flow of loss for her parents, but she does not know how. She has her own loss. "I don't really talk to anyone in my family," she says. "Trang is the closest person to me on earth. She was my lifetime companion, my friend—my sister."

It is up to Thao now to take care of a mother who does not speak English or know how the strange country works. For Trang, "family was the most important thing—after that her education and lifetime goals." But Thao feels more conflicted about familial obligations—she has a boyfriend and wants to forge a life of her own. When her parents' troubles began she says, "I had stepped back and Trang had taken over. Now that she's gone, it's overwhelming again. I can't replace Trang. In my parents' hearts she's their hope. I can't talk about her with them."

Mother's Day that year—close to the anniversary of Trang's death—had been a terrible day for her mother. Thao gave her a card from her and Tram. But Trang was the one who always did things like that—buying her mother roses, writing cards on the three girls' behalf. Before her death Trang had planned to be a doctor, Tram a lawyer, and Thao a psychiatrist or a social worker. "I'd tease my mom that she'd have everyone to take care of her," Thao says. But Thao no longer believes in their dreams. She plans to go back to school and study accounting. She doesn't think she will enjoy it, but she won't have to be in school that long, and it will be practical and support the family.

Thao says that she thinks she believes Trang is in heaven. Trang was a Buddhist, she says, but she also believed you could control your own destiny. She dreams about Trang; she feels her presence in her life. "For her to die is so unfair," she says. "I wonder: Why don't you take me? Trang really has a lot going on for her."

When I tell her that her life is valuable too, she says, "But I think I live enough—I don't really care, I wish I could take her place and let her live."

Thao says that part of her feels angry at Sinedu, but part of her also thinks: Maybe she really needs help and there wasn't anyone for her. Trang said in the beginning Sinedu was a nice person.

The family has tried to avoid the press, which has often harassed them. Shortly after the death a reporter asked Thao's boyfriend to try to get the family to talk to him, explaining that he needed quotes from the family to make his story more "colorful." Reporters always ask how they feel about Harvard, but they don't know what to say. People tell them Harvard should give them some kind of settlement, but, Thao says, "we can't expect them to do something they don't want to."

Harvard never told the Ho family that the school did an internal investigation after the death, or what the results of that investigation were. "We don't know anything," Thao says. Suzi Naiburg, the Dunster House senior tutor, was given the role of being the liaison for the family. She would call them up occasionally and ask how they were doing, but "What are we supposed to say?" Thao says. "We're not fine?" They don't ask her questions because they don't want to "put her in a situation between us and Harvard. It would be very uncomfortable for her. She has a hard job."

They don't recall Naiburg mentioning that she knew Trang, or that—as Naiburg told the police—Trang had been to see her to talk about her rooming problems at the end of her life. Naiburg invited the family to attend commencement the following year, but she told them that Trang would not be mentioned during the ceremony. They declined, so she sent them a tape of commencement instead, which they could never bring themselves to watch. "Usually at graduation they mention the members of the class who have died, don't they?" Thao says.

Harvard is very aggressive when it comes to the threat of publicity: when NBC approached the Ho family about doing a program on Trang, Suzi Naiburg promptly called the family and Trang's friend Jim Igoe, warning them against cooperation. "We just don't want to see the family manipulated," she told Jim Igoe.

"Does she think we're stupid?" Jim Igoe said. "Who is manipulating who? They just want Trang to be forgotten."

Since Trang's death, Jim Igoe has acted as an advocate for the family. The family wanted to bring Trang's grandparents over from Vietnam to comfort their daughter and see their granddaughter's grave. Jim kept calling Harvard to try to get help with travel funds and visas, but, he says, he kept "hitting a brick wall." Every official he called would refer him to another official or not return his calls. Massachusetts Senator John Kerry's office, on the other hand, was much more responsive. Finally Jim spoke to a *Boston Globe* reporter, and an acerbic column, with a headline of "Grief Compounded by Indifference," stated that "for two months Harvard turned a deaf ear" and that "only the certainty of public disclosure" prompted a belated offer of help. Just before the anniversary of Trang's death, aided by Harvard and Senator Kerry's office, Trang's grandparents arrived. Jim Igoe is still working to obtain permanent residency for them; he has recently applied to be their sponsor, guaranteeing the government he will provide for them financially when in need.

A woman at the temple says that Trang must have done something to Sinedu in another life—otherwise why else would they have ended up rooming together? And to happen at Harvard too; it would make no sense. We are all in unfinished relationships from previous lives, she said; as soon as she met her husband, she knew they had known each other for a long time. Trang must have done something very wrong to Sinedu to have died in such a way. The Buddha is very fair; everything is a balancing out.

Did Trang's parents do something wrong in their previous life, I ask, that they deserve to have a daughter die? No, no, she tells me impatiently: life is suffering. Children die. Her parents need to accept that Trang had spent all the time with them that she had to spend.

"If you want to bring a picture of Sinedu," she adds, gesturing toward the table, "we will pray for her too."

Thao Nguyen has not healed from the attack. She has had two operations, but she still needs a skin graft over the gash that covers most of her tiny hand. She has medical bills to pay, which Harvard has not helped her with. The news office told *The New Yorker*'s fact checker that Harvard had offered to pay, and Thao hadn't responded, but Thao says she never received any such offer. And she won't ask—even after I tell her what they said— because she does not want to ask for money connected to her friend's death.

She is haunted by self-reproach that she did not try to get the knife from Sinedu a second time. I tell her that Detective Dwyer told me that "Thao did an incredible job trying to save her friend and should be commended," but she is unconvinced. She says, "Trang always tell me I so strong because of all I came through in Vietnam—why then I not save Trang?" She calls Trang's mother sometimes, but the sound of her voice makes Quy cry. Once when she called Quy cried, "Why did you leave Trang in the room?" Thao knows she doesn't mean it, but it still makes her feel terrible.

In Vietnamese culture, the spirit of the dead return in dreams. On the operating table, Thao dreamed about Trang and woke with the sense that Trang was angry with her. For months afterward in her dreams she would ask Trang to forgive her, but she would also tell her that she understood if Trang didn't want to because she had run away when Trang was being killed. In the dreams, though, Trang would never reply to her. Once Thao dreamed she was climbing up a mountain, carrying an unbearably heavy bundle. She could see Trang ahead of her, across a stream, and she called to her and hurried to catch up. But when she reached the stream and tried to give Trang the bundle, Trang turned away from her and Thao had to continue up the mountain alone.

In Vietnam, when Thao was a child, her beloved sister Truc, with whom she shared a room, fell sick. Thao and her younger brothers were sent away to visit their aunt in Saigon for the weekend. When she returned, her mother told her that Truc had been apprenticed to a priest and had gone to live at a temple. Thao would cry at nights, missing her sister, but she would picture her in the temple, living her life somewhere else. Years later, she found pictures of the funeral. When she came to America, she told Trang about her sister and Trang said, "I am your sister now."

"I believe my sister follow me and help me," she says. "A lot of times I think I'm not going to make it, but I did—I think Trang must be my sister—the way she talk and share with me—she understand me even though we just know each other for one year." Truc had died early in the year in 1975; Trang was born in April of that same year. Thao remembers how, after Trang slept over at Thao's apartment, Trang would leave her friend a hidden note, which Thao would find several days later, telling her that she was strong or good or that Trang loved her. Trang befriended her when she first came to America; Thao still needs her, but she can stand on her own. "It's like she finish a job with me and now she gone," she says.

Thao cannot believe that Trang had ever done anything wrong—even in another life—because "she so good. There is no one in the world who perfect, but she perfect." In Buddhist philosophy, sometimes people die to pay for their sins, but sometimes they die because they have nothing to pay for anymore and are just ready to move on.

Thao thinks Trang died so that "she didn't have to live the sad life—sometimes she was happy, but most of the time she was sad because she have a lot of things to worry about—her sister, her mother, her father, their future." She knows Trang is in paradise now, as the reverend says, but she says, "Maybe I'm selfish, but I still want her to be reborn." I ask how she pictures Trang reborn, and she says, "As a Vietnamese girl in America, very successful. She continue what she left and be a doctor, helping people, just like she always want to do." She had a dream in which Trang was away, but she missed her friends and exams and graduation and wanted to know if she could return, or if she had missed too much to make up, and Thao reassured her that it is not too late, she could still come back, there is still a place for her here.

Finally Thao dreamed she was standing alone in a room and Trang came up to her from behind and put her arms around her and said, "I know you're so lonely now that I'm leaving you." Thao said, "Ya, I'm so lonely." Thao had always loved Trang's hands; she had reached for them in the coffin, but gloves had been put on to cover the wounds. But in the dream Thao takes Trang's hands and they are smooth and whole again and Thao knows that Trang loves and forgives her. "I know Trang she really love me," she says, "I know she forgive me."

For a long time Thao was very angry at Sinedu. "How could she?" she would ask again and again whenever we talked. "How could she?" She would write in her diary that she hated Sinedu and her family and her country, but then she would be frightened that Sinedu might know and try to hurt her again. The police told her that the reason Sinedu killed Trang is "not because they were fighting, not because of Trang, but because she have long time problem in her mind, she think she very alone and have no one." But Thao has had a hard life herself. "Sometimes I am very alone. I can't tell my parents my problems because they have too hard a life—sometimes I go crazy, I want to kill myself, but I never did anything."

She thinks there were two people in Sinedu—one was nice and polite and quiet, the way Thao had always seen her, but also arrogant, and the other "really bad like a beast." When the arrogant person saw Trang had more family and friends than she did, the beast took over and made her become a killer. "If she alive now," Thao says, "maybe Sinedu couldn't believe what she had done and maybe she knew she would feel that, and that is why she killed herself."

After many months Thao has a dream about Sinedu. In the dream Sinedu stood at the end of her bed in the darkness. Sinedu didn't say anything, but she tried to look at her and she touched Thao's leg in a way that made Thao understand that she is sorry now.

"Maybe she couldn't help herself," Thao tells me in a soft voice. I know that the quality that enables Thao to believe that Trang loves her—the belief that she is loved and loving—is something that Sinedu had never had, though she sought it all her life; and it seems therefore a kind of final truth: Sinedu actually could not help herself.

M t. Auburn, where Trang is buried, is an immense beautiful nineteenth century cemetery, where Henry Wadsworth Longfellow, Mary Baker Eddy, and generations of Harvard dignitaries and elite Bostonians lie. A dozen people gather with the Reverend Dr. Thich Giac Duc for the first-anniversary ceremony of Trang's death—Trang's mother and sisters, Thao and Tram, Jim Igoe, Thao Nguyen, Khoi Luu, and other friends of Trang's I don't recognize. Suzi Naiburg is there as well, carrying a potted plant.

My friend Bibi's funeral had been held at Mt. Auburn Cemetery as well, on a bitter December day in 1984—the year Trang arrived in a refugee camp in Indonesia and began to learn English. I always thought I would go back to visit her grave, but I never did. She died, as Trang did, without knowing why. Her body was found in the forest, her head smashed in with a rock. Her boyfriend was convicted, but he went to jail saying he was innocent. I thought one day I would find out what happened, but I no longer believe that I will.

Hundreds of mourners had attended Trang's funeral a year ago, looking on while the saffron-robed priest clanged bells and burned incense and chanted in Vietnamese, Chinese, and Sanskrit. When the chanting ceased the reverend had looked up and translated: "Ladies and gentlemen. Life is impermanence. We are as tiny dust. Life subject to destruction. Life full of sorrow. Death cause sorrow. Love and separation cause sorrow. Hate cause sorrow. Hatred, greed, and ignorance make a man violent and violence cause more sorrow. We must cultivate peaceful mind and peaceful manner and not follow way of violence, but practice love and compassion towards friend and foe."

When Trang's mother's cries became too loud to bear, the reverend stopped the service and placed his hand on her forehead, trying to give her peaceful energy. Life is not short, but long, he told her: we live from sunrise to sunset, but within that impermanence there is something permanent.

From the chapel the mourners made their way to the grave site, where the dark casket gleamed in the May morning beside the newly broken ground. The family circled the coffin three times to the sound of drumbeats, escorting Trang into a new life. Male relatives carried Quy, too weak to walk. The coffin was lowered into the earth and each family member dropped a flower down. Trang's mother wavered before the nest of the grave, as if she might fall. One by one Trang's relatives, friends, members of the temple, teachers, the president of Harvard, and other officials lined up before the grave. Dressed in white Vietnamese mourning garb, Thao Nguyen carried a long-stemmed rose, her face tear-stained, her hand and foot swaddled in bandages.

There had been a dancelike quality to the procession, moving silently and rhythmically forward, as one by one people dropped their flowers onto the shiny black casket. I had wanted to join them, but I stood back where the press had been gathered, uncertain.

Now, as the anniversary ceremony concludes, I start to leave with the others, but I had told myself that this time I would visit Bibi's grave. I walk back to the guard station at the gate and ask the attendant how to find it, but he can't find the book which lists the graves for that year, though the years surrounding it are all there. He shrugs, half embarrassed. They say that everything we once knew we always know, somewhere in our mind, and I remember that day so clearly—standing with the other mourners in a semicircle in the falling snow, numbed by the sound of Chinese—that I decide to wander around and see if I can find my way to it.

I walk for a long time through the labyrinth of plots and flowering hedges, birds calling to each other in every direction, but it's Trang's grave I find I have made my way back to. The earth has closed over now, the gravestone inlaid, flat as a jewel. I remember the grave at the funeral, the tear-shaped blossoms sifting slowly down over the onyx casket. I pluck a flower and stand staring down at the grave. The reality of the loss is so overwhelming that all reflection seems to collapse into a sense of inevitability: Sinedu was possessed by spirits or psychosis; Trang was perfected and ready to enter into the Pure Land; Harvard didn't foresee and couldn't prevent anything.

"Pessimism doesn't change the world," Trang told her high school class in her valedictory speech. "You decide where your life is going, whether you are going to make a difference or not. For me, I will make many differences."

Her words drift downward like falling flowers.

Notes

1. *At The Crossroads: The Future of Foreign Aid* (Silver Spring, Maryland: Bread for the World Institute, 1995).

2. The most recent is a study of suicides on the big ten university campuses, to be published in late 1997, by Morton M. Silverman, director of the University of Chicago student counseling service.

3. "Almost one-half of the suicide completers were seen as definitely or probably conceiving of their deaths as 'a way to get even with someone.' " Ronald W. Maris, "Social Relations of Suicide," *Suicide: Understanding and Responding, Harvard Medical School Perspectives,* Douglas Jacobs, M.D., and Herbert N. Brown, M.D., eds. (Madison, Conn.: International Universities Press, 1989).

4. Peter M. Marzuk, M.D., Kenneth Tardiff, M.D., M.Ph.; Charles S. Hirsch, M.D., "The Epidemiology of Murder-Suicide," *The Journal of the American Medical Association,* June 17, 1992.

5. *National Committee on Traditional Practices in Ethiopia* (Addis Ababa, Ethiopia: Addis Ababa University Printing Press, 1995).

Acknowledgments

First of all I want to thank my saintly editors, Henry Finder at *The New Yorker*, who gave me the assignment on faith and saw me through it, and Betsy Lerner at Doubleday—a gifted editor and a perfect match—and her assistant, Laura Hodes.

To my agent, Henry Dunow—all that an agent should be.

I am greatly indebted to many mental health professionals who gave me their time and insight: Susan Besharov, Margaret Chisolm, Margaret Dieter, Elizabeth Fagan, Aleme Feyissa, Tedla Wolde Giorgis, Ruth Graver, Sandra Green, Henry, Judy, and Michael Grunebaum, Dennis Haseley, Elliot Jurist, James Longhurst, Paul McHugh, Sandra Siler, and James Traub.

Thanks to First Assistant District Attorney Martin Murphy, who headed the homicide investigation, for his generosity with his time and expertise.

To Leon Friedman, Ann Pauly, and Katherine Trager for expert legal advice.

To the Edward Albee Foundation in Montauk, New York.

To Tsegaye Arrefe, Tizita Belachew, Laura Blumenfeld, Elie Kaunfer, Camille Paglia, Thomas Palmer, and especially Timothy Sultan for their help.

In a book about the necessity of friendship, I am blessed by friends who are good critics as well as good friends, and who took time from their own work to read and improve this manuscript line by line: Cynthia Baughman, David Edelstein, Darcy Frey, Herschel Garfein, Elizabeth Graver, Brian Hall, Julie Hilden, Claudia Kolker, Christopher MacDougall, Richard Moran, Tom Reiss, Dani Shapiro, Nicholas Weinstock and especially Nicholas Dawidoff, without whom I never would have turned to journalism.

Thanks to my parents, Stephan and Abigail.

And thanks most of all to the people in the book whose story it is and who took the risk of letting me tell it.

About the Author

Melanie Thernstrom is the author of *The Dead Girl*. A native of Boston, she graduated from Harvard University in 1987 and has taught writing at Cornell, Harvard, and Boston University. Her journalism has appeared in *The New Yorker*. She lives in New York City.